P9-ELV-869

English FOR EVERYDAY LIVING

Nell Stiglitz Reitman

Language Arts Teacher, Bremen High School, Midlothian, Illinois
B.A. in Liberal Arts, University of Illinois
LL.B., Northwestern University
Graduate Studies in English, University of Notre Dame
Graduate Studies in Special Education, National College of Education

Sally Shapiro Pellati

Head of English Department, Washington Junior High School, Chicago Heights, Illinois
B.S. in Education, Northern Illinois University
Graduate Studies in English, Indiana University, National College of Education, Chicago State University

IDEAL PUBLICATIONS

A Division of Ideal School Supply Company
11000 South Lavergne Avenue, Oak Lawn, Illinois 60453
A SERVICE OF WESTINGHOUSE LEARNING CORPORATION

11000 South Lavergne Avenue, Oak Lawn, Illinois 60453
Eleventh Printing

Printed in the United States of America
ISBN Number: 0-89099-429-3

ACKNOWLEDGEMENTS

P. 10	Symbols courtesy of Morton Salt Co., Illinois Bell, Western Publishing Co., Inc.
P. 43	National Park Service
P. 48, 50	U.S. Government Printing Office
P. 49	Architect of the Capital
P. 51	Bureau of Engraving and Printing
P. 76	G. Becker
P. 77	American Cancer Society
P. 78	New York Convention and Visitors Bureau
P. 85	Cunard Line Ltd.
P. 108	United States Post Office
P. 114–116	Montgomery Ward
P. 119–120	Social Security Administration
P. 124–125	Carson, Pirie, Scott and Co.
P. 127–129	U.S. Department of State
P. 131	Illinois Department of Labor
P. 133–136	Illinois Department of Public Aid
P. 149	Material from the *Reader's Guide to Periodical Literature* is reproduced by permission of the H. W. Wilson Co.
P. 150–164	*Chicago Tribune*
P. 155	Brenda Starr, Lolly, Broom-Hilda, and Gasoline Alley reprinted by permission of the *Chicago Tribune*. All rights reserved. Moon Mullins reprinted by permission of the New York News, Inc. All rights reserved.
P. 157	*Chicago Sun Times*
P. 158	New Trier West High School, Northfield, Ill.
P. 167	Clairol, Inc.
P. 178, 180	M. T. Arnold
P. 198, 210	National Aeronautics and Space Administration

FOREWORD

ENGLISH FOR EVERYDAY LIVING is a book designed for young adults to help in mastering those techniques that are vital to success in coping with our present day world.

Too often, these functional and rudimentary skills are taken for granted, while the student is actually becoming mired in a morass of terms and expressions that hold little or no real meaning or interest.

If one subscribes to the premise that life becomes easier when English is simplified, then this book with its practical vocabulary and high interest content, will fulfill this need.

BENJAMIN L. BRAUN
Director of Special Education
Southwest Cook County Cooperative
Association for Special Education

CONTENTS

English
FOR
EVERYDAY LIVING

Chapter ONE

DO I KNOW . . .

WHO AM I?

As young adults in high school, we have definite ideas about ourselves, others, and our lives. Knowing who we are and who other people are is important.

People are not all alike, and their feelings and opinions are often very different. On a separate sheet of paper, complete the following sentences.

Thinking About School

1. High school is ______________________________.
2. When I bring my semester grades home ______________.
3. Some teachers are ______________________________.
4. I like teachers who ______________________________.
5. It bothers me when teachers ______________________.
6. Lunch in the cafeteria is ________________________.
7. I am happy at school when ________________________.
8. My favorite class is ____________________________.
9. Instead of tennis, I would rather ________________.
10. Someday I will graduate and _______________________.

Thinking About My Family

1. My family is ______________________________.
2. My mother is ______________________________.
3. My home is ______________________________.
4. My father is ______________________________.
5. I wish my father would ______________________.
6. A sister is ______________________________.
7. A brother is ______________________________.
8. I stay home from school when __________________.
9. I wish my mother would _______________________.
10. When I was very small, I liked __________________.

Thinking About Myself

1. I hope someday I will ______________________.
2. I get angry when ______________________.
3. If nobody helps me, I ______________________.
4. I do my best when I ______________________.
5. I hope I never will ______________________.
6. I am unhappy when ______________________.
7. My friends don't know that I ______________________.
8. If only I could ______________________.
9. I hate ______________________.
10. I like to be alone when ______________________.

DISCUSSING REAL LIFE SITUATIONS

It is good to talk about how we think and feel. This helps others to understand us and helps us understand others. Talking about real life happenings is called a discussion.

Think about these questions. Talk about your feelings and ideas.

1. What is a good life?
2. What can I do to make my family, my teachers, and others happy? Unhappy?
3. What have I done that made somebody happy?
4. Would I help someone in trouble?
5. Do I think only about myself?
6. What have I done that made someone dislike me?
7. What things have I done that make me proud of myself?
8. What is something that I want very much? Why do I want it?
9. What one thing would I like to change about myself?
10. What do I like best about myself?

WHAT WOULD YOU DO IF . . .

To imagine is to make believe. We don't always know how we might act if we were to find ourselves in a specific situation. Let's imagine that the following situations happened. Write two or three sentences to tell how you think the person in the story would handle each of these situations. Write your answers on a separate sheet of paper.

1. Joe Garallo came up to Robert in school and told him that he had some marijuana. Robert should come to Joe's house after school, if he wants to try it.

Joe said, "My dad doesn't get home till 2:00 a.m., so we have the house to ourselves."

Should Robert go to Joe's house? Tell why or why not.

2. Emily sits behind Mary in math class. They are taking a test on fractions.

"Work as many problems as you can. I have to go to the office, but I'll be right back," says Mr. Morris, the math teacher. When Mr. Morris leaves the room, Mary holds up her paper, and Emily quickly writes down several answers.

Sara has studied hard for this test and is upset when she sees Emily cheating. Would Sara tell Mr. Morris? Why or why not? When would she tell him?

3. "Where's your semester grade card, Jim?" asked Craig. "It's in my gym locker—I'm not taking it home. My parents would ground me for the whole semester if they saw my grades."

Should Jim take his semester grades home? Why or why not?

Look at your answers to the above situations. The following questions will help you check your writing.

1. Do all the sentences start with capital letters?
2. Do all the sentences have punctuation marks at the ends?
3. Can other people read the writing?
4. Do the sentences make sense?

HOW DO OTHERS AFFECT ME?

We are not alone in our world. There are times when we need help. Everyone needs someone's help at some time in his or her life. Today's world has special people who can help in different ways. For example, there are many kinds of doctors, who can help you in different ways.

Medical Professions

Match the following doctors with their specialties listed on the opposite page. Write your answers on a separate sheet of paper. Who would you call if . . .

______ 1. you need a family doctor?

______ 2. you have a toothache?

______ 3. your teeth need to be straightened?

______ 4. you need an operation?

______ 5. ether is needed for an operation?

______ 6. your sister is pregnant?

______ 7. your child is sick?

______ 8. your feet are sore?

______ 9. your skin breaks out in a rash?

______ 10. a person has a heart attack?

______ 11. a person has a problem with mental health?

______ 12. a person suffers from severe mental illness?

______ 13. you need glasses?

______ 14. you need an x-ray?

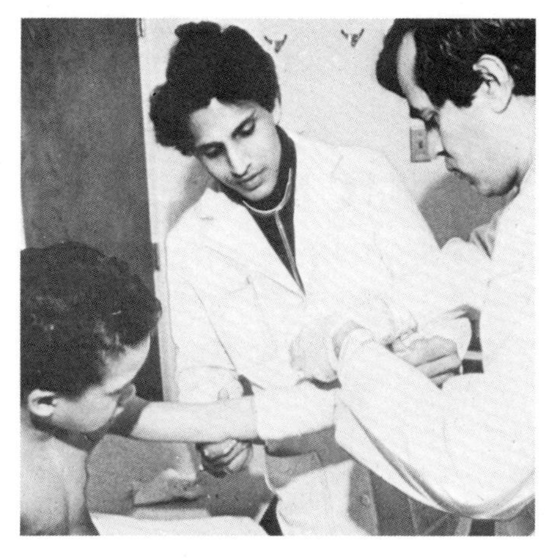

PEDIATRICIAN

OPTOMETRIST

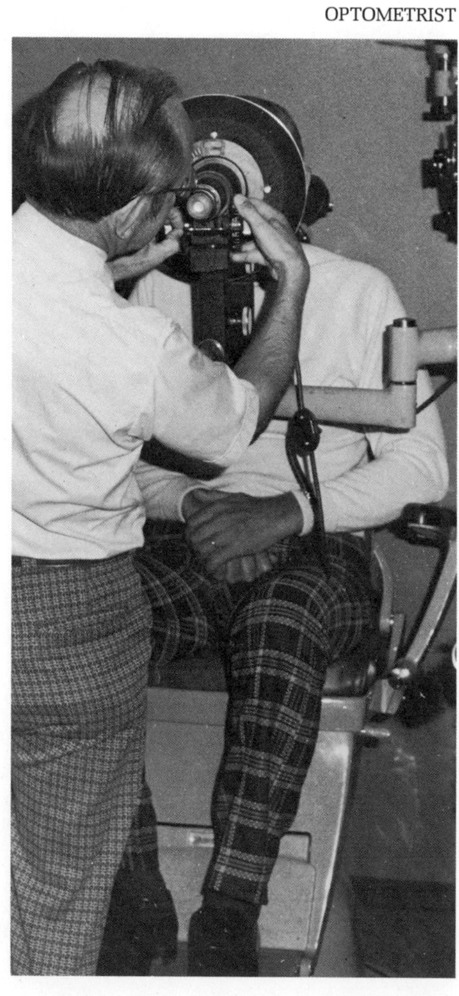

a. obstetrician

b. podiatrist

c. pediatrician

d. orthodontist

e. dermatologist

f. general practitioner

g. cardiologist

h. psychiatrist

i. surgeon

j. psychologist

k. optometrist

l. dentist

m. radiologist

n. anesthetist

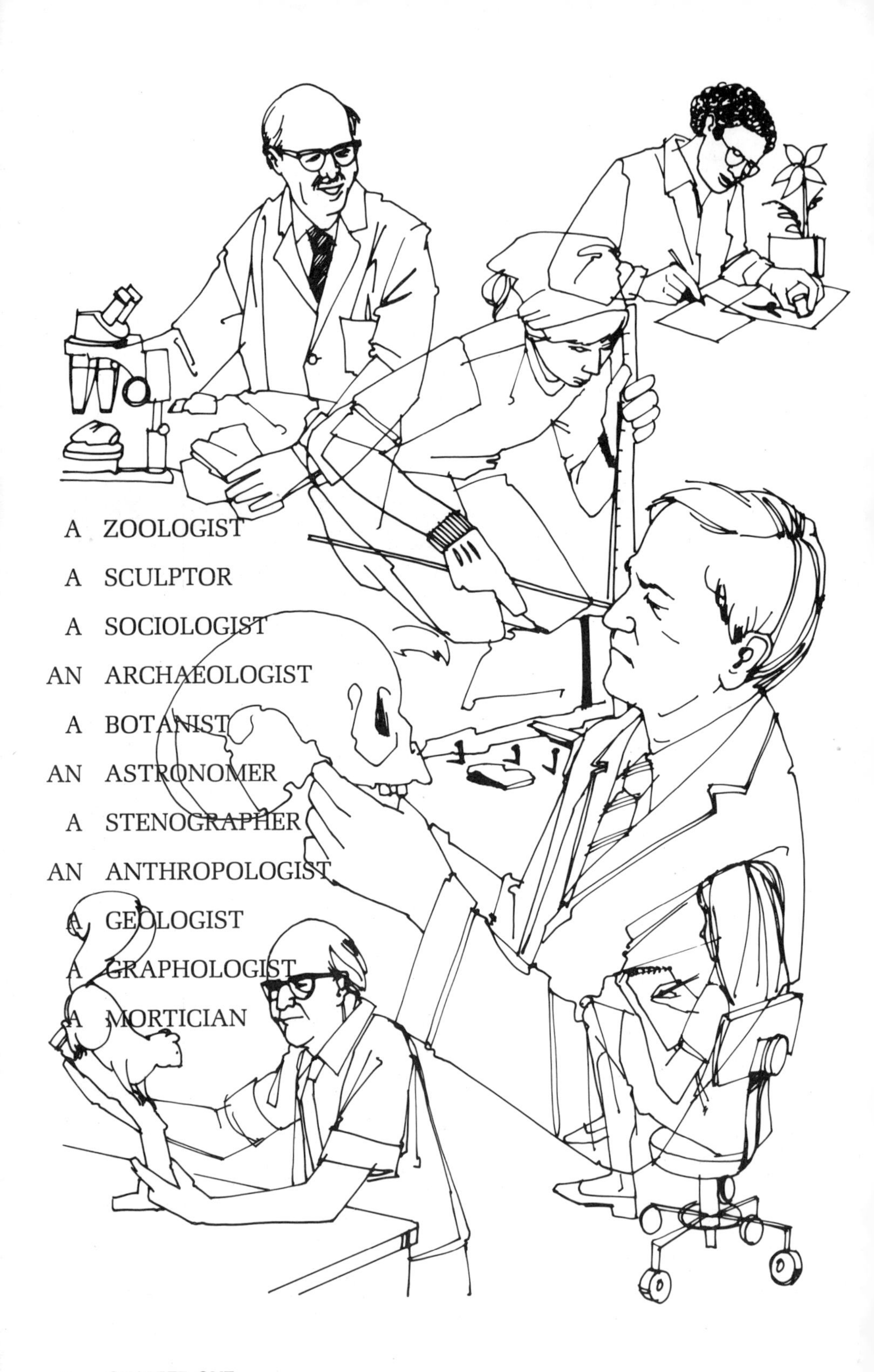
A ZOOLOGIST
A SCULPTOR
A SOCIOLOGIST
AN ARCHAEOLOGIST
A BOTANIST
AN ASTRONOMER
A STENOGRAPHER
AN ANTHROPOLOGIST
A GEOLOGIST
A GRAPHOLOGIST
A MORTICIAN

Occupations

There are specialists in almost every kind of work today. Can you match the specialists (listed on page 8) with their occupations? Write your answers on a separate sheet of paper.

1. A person who studies animals is called ________________.
2. A person who studies plants is called ________________.
3. A person who studies people and their surroundings is called ________________.
4. A person who studies about the development of human life is called ________________.
5. A person who studies about people from the past and ancient civilizations is called ________________.
6. A person who studies natural resources, particularly rocks, is called ________________.
7. A person who studies the sun, moon, stars, and planets is called ________________.
8. A person who studies how handwriting reveals a person's character is called ________________.
9. A person who prepares dead bodies for burial is called ________________.
10. A person who is skilled in typing and shorthand is called ________________.
11. A person who makes figures from clay or stone is called ________________.

Chapter TWO

HOW DO I COMMUNICATE?

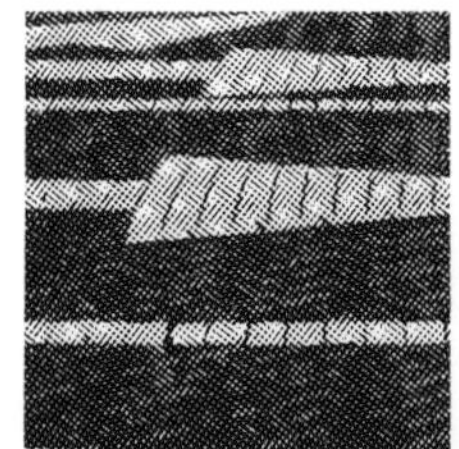
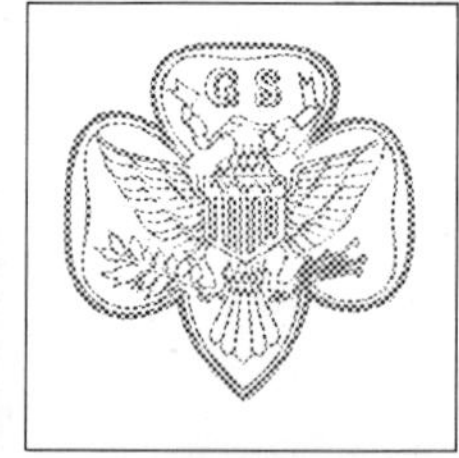

COMMUNICATING WITHOUT WORDS

Imagine someone who is angry. Often a person doesn't have to say anything to show angry feelings. A person's actions or the look on a person's face will often tell others what the person is feeling. Angry people can move their hands or their entire bodies in a way that shows that they are angry. These and many other clues can tell us how a person feels.

You tell others how you feel by the look on your face and by your body movements. Sometimes, you may not want others to know how you feel, but the look on your face shows your feelings. If you are unhappy about something, you might frown. If your teacher calls on you when you don't know the answer, you might shrug your shoulders. When something is boring, you might yawn.

Can you communicate with someone without using words? How can you show someone you're happy? How can you show someone you're sad?

GESTURES, BODY MOTIONS

Hand or body motions are called gestures. We can use gestures to show that something is tall. We can tell someone, without using words, that there is something that we like and that we want it. We can also show when there is something that we don't like, and that we don't want it. Tears, smiles, the ways we hold our bodies, and the ways we sit, walk, and run can show how we feel. Without using any words at all, we can make clear to other people many different feelings and thoughts. We can communicate without words.

If you used each of the following gestures, what would you be trying to tell another person? Tell what you would communicate if you...

1. put your fingers across your lips.
2. put your hand behind your ear.
3. nod your head up and down; shake your head left and right.
4. wave your hand.
5. stick your tongue out.
6. clap your hands.
7. tap your feet.
8. close your fist tightly.

TONE

In addition to gestures, people also show feelings by the tone of their voices. People use a soft tone of voice to make a baby happy. Some babies cry when they hear a harsh tone. Circus trainers give sharp and rough commands when working with animals. No matter what language circus trainers use, the commands are understood because of their tone of voice.

ANIMAL COMMUNICATION

Animals cannot understand words, but they do understand the tone of our voices. Dogs know by the tone of our voices when to run, when to hide, and when to come to us. Dogs also communicate with us. They rub against our legs to show affection. They wag their tails to show they're happy. And, when they're afraid, they lower their ears and tails.

Animals—and even the smallest insects—have ways of communicating with each other. Ants communicate with their antennae. Fish change their color to show fear or anger. A baby bird will hold its mouth wide open when it is hungry. Then, the parent bird will stuff food into the baby bird's mouth. A male crab waves a claw to attract a female crab. Animals, like people, need to communicate. All animals have a special system of communication.

SIGNS AND SYMBOLS

Sometimes, it is easiest and most effective to communicate with pictures. Color, shape, and design are used to get the message across—surely and quickly. Traffic signs try to prevent accidents. All drivers know that a red octagon is a stop sign.

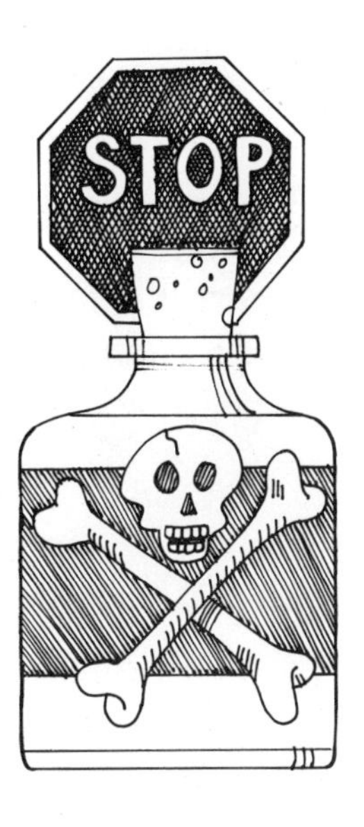

Symbols are also used to stand for a specific place, idea, or thing. Parents teach young children the symbol for poison. It's important for children to understand the message DANGER whenever they see a skull and crossbones.

Some symbols suggest or represent certain ideas or qualities. The symbol of a lion is used to represent bravery, a heart suggests love, an owl suggests wisdom.

Sometimes, people like to use symbols as a kind of identification. Countries usually have an official symbol which is often used as their flag. There are symbols for political parties, too. Do you know what these symbols stand for?

Symbols and signs are important ways to communicate without words. Many messages can be understood quickly and easily.

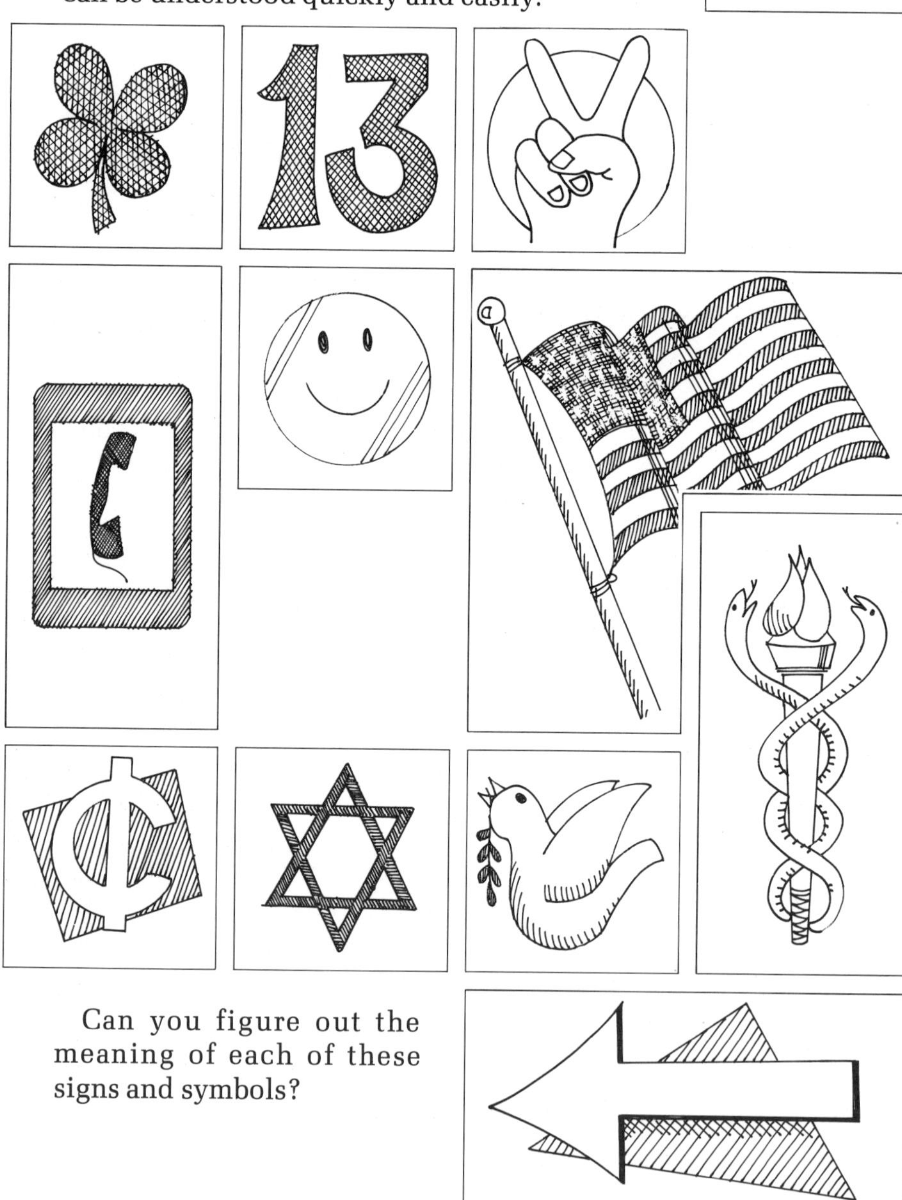

Can you figure out the meaning of each of these signs and symbols?

WORDS

Words are a kind of symbol, too. Words stand for specific objects and ideas. The word *car* is the symbol for a kind of vehicle. The word *dog* is the symbol for a kind of pet.

Our English language and many other languages, such as French, Italian, Spanish, and German, are made up of symbols which stand for sounds. We call these symbols letters. By putting the sounds together, we make words.

PICTURE WRITING

A few languages, such as Chinese and Japanese, do not use letters. They use pictures to communicate. These pictures will often have different meanings in different areas of the country.

Egyptian tombs contain another example of picture writing. This picture writing is called hieroglyphics (hī′-ra-glĭf′ĭks). The pictures were used to tell stories of how people lived, the things they did, and their feelings about their world. The ancient Egyptians did not have letters to combine to form words. Instead, they drew pictures.

EGYPTIAN HIEROGLYPHICS

CHINESE CHARACTERS

On a separate sheet of paper, do the following:

1. Draw pictures of five different objects. Do not use any words.
2. Draw some pictures to show a feeling, like sadness, love, or fear.
3. Try to say something by putting pictures together, without using any words.
4. Figure out what this picture writing means.

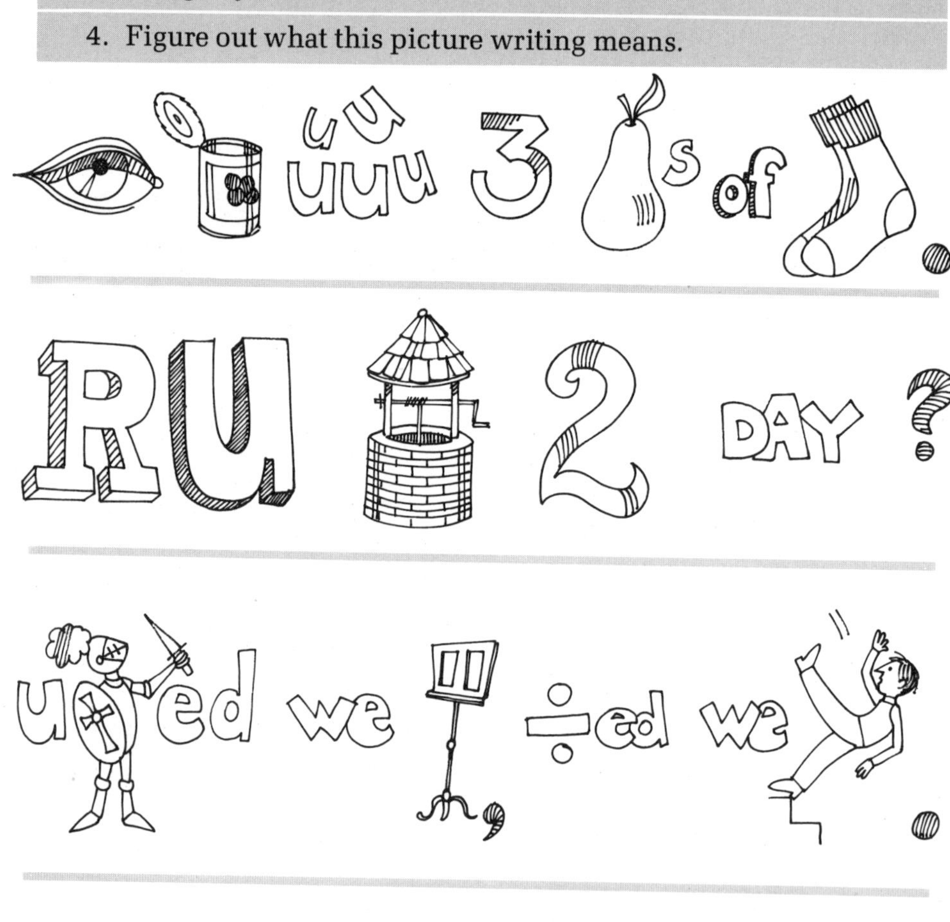

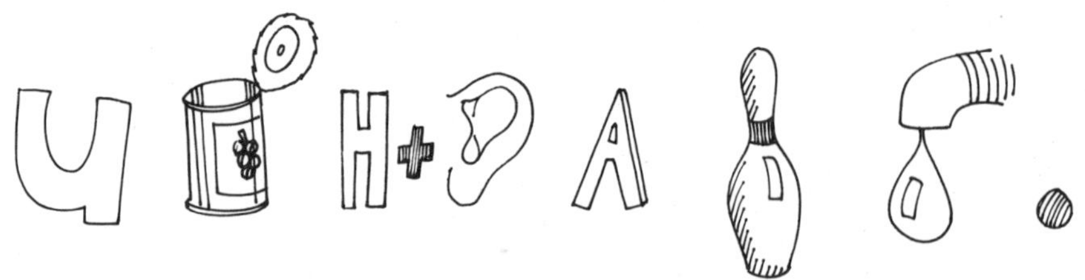

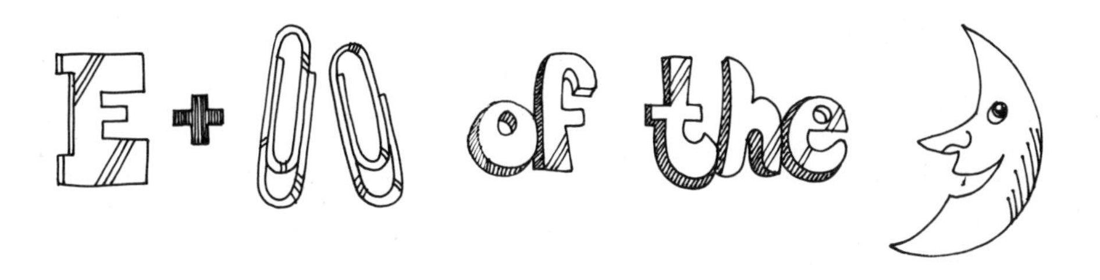

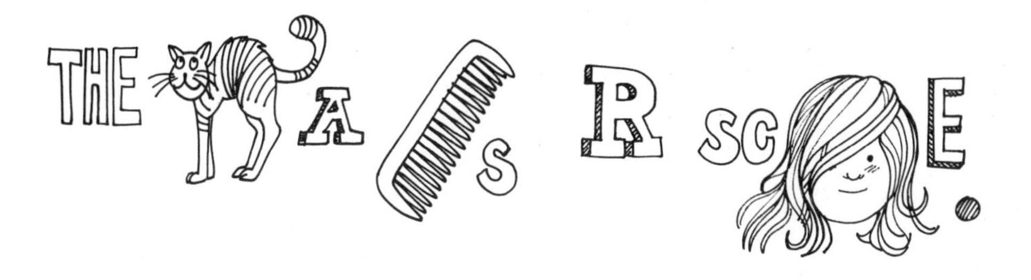

THE WRITTEN AND SPOKEN WORD

We have discussed many different ways of communication. People most often use writing and speaking to communicate. People read and write notes, letters, stories, and books everyday. And every day people talk about ideas and feelings.

It is important to say exactly what we mean when we write or speak. There are rules to follow to communicate effectively. These rules are explained in the chapters of this book. Read the rules, practice using them, and enjoy using the written and spoken word correctly!

Chapter THREE

DO I UNDERSTAND THE SPECIALIZED ENGLISH SKILLS?

A person who knows how to use words has power. Word power can grow and grow. The secret is learning a few skills.

PREFIXES

How can you make a word grow? Look! Add letters to the beginning of a word and watch it grow.

mis	+	spell	=	misspell
re	+	turn	=	return
un	+	happy	=	unhappy
semi	+	sweet	=	semisweet
sub	+	way	=	subway
fore	+	head	=	forehead
pre	+	school	=	preschool
im	+	proper	=	improper
bi	+	weekly	=	biweekly
trans	+	world	=	transworld
anti	+	war	=	antiwar

A syllable or syllables added to the beginning of a word is called a prefix. "Pre" means before, and a prefix is letters fixed or added before or at the beginning of a word. The word to which the prefix is added is called a root word.

The following list describes some common prefixes and their meanings. Learning the meanings of prefixes can help your vocabulary grow and help you figure out new words.

mis	=	wrong	*fore*	=	before
re	=	back or again	*pre*	=	before
un	=	not	*im*	=	not
semi	=	half	*bi*	=	two or twice
sub	=	under	*trans*	=	across

Here are some root words. Copy them onto a separate sheet of paper. Then, make them grow by adding prefixes from the list on page 19.

1. ______________ kind	6. ______________ view
2. ______________ conduct	7. ______________ polite
3. ______________ place	8. ______________ circle
4. ______________ cycle	9. ______________ word
5. ______________ way	10. ______________ plant

SUFFIXES

Now, let's make words grow at the other end. Syllables added to the ends of root words are called suffixes.

care	+	*ful*	=	careful
comfort	+	*able*	=	comfortable
hope	+	*less*	=	hopeless
child	+	*ish*	=	childish
soft	+	*en*	=	soften
work	+	*er*	=	worker
conduct	+	*or*	=	conductor
adult	+	*hood*	=	adulthood
home	+	*ward*	=	homeward

These are some common suffixes and their meanings. Learning the meanings of suffixes can help your vocabulary grow and help you figure out new words.

less	=	without	*er, or*	=	one who
able	=	able to be	*hood*	=	state of being
ish	=	like	*ward*	=	in the direction of
en	=	to make	*ful*	=	filled with

Here are some root words. Copy them onto a separate sheet of paper. Then, make them grow by adding suffixes from the list on the bottom of page 20.

1. brother ________________	7. soft ________________
2. dark ________________	8. help ________________
3. cheer ________________	9. west ________________
4. speak ________________	10. fear ________________
5. thank ________________	11. fool ________________
6. talk ________________	12. change ________________

Notice–There are some cases when you must drop a final **e** *to add a suffix.*

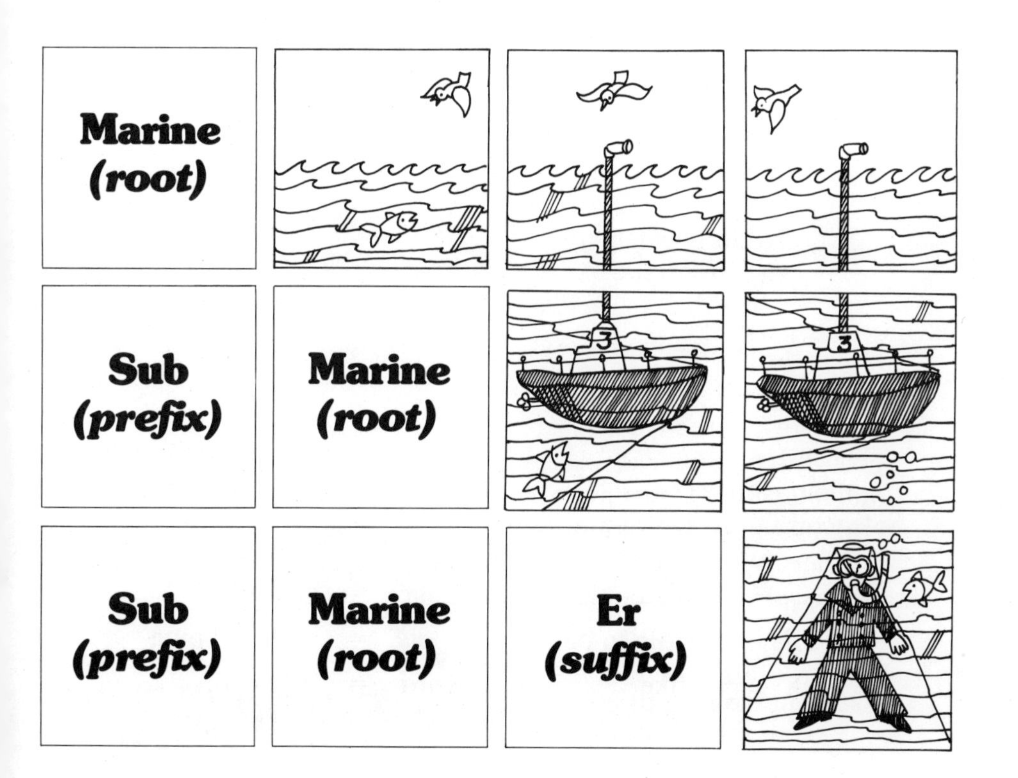

Practice Using Prefixes and Suffixes

Now make the root word grow from each end. Copy these root words onto a separate sheet of paper. Add both a prefix and a suffix from those listed below to each root word.

Prefix *pre, re, un*	**Root**	**Suffix** *er, ness, able*
pre	school	er
________	view	________
________	kind	________
________	turn	________
________	believe	________
________	place	________
________	comfort	________
________	form	________
________	print	________
________	use	________
________	accept	________

Notice—There are some cases when you must drop a final **e** *to add a suffix.*

As we grow, we understand more. But, can others understand us? Using just the right word can be a big help to others as well as to yourself. People will know exactly what you mean. You will be able to communicate your ideas and feelings to others.

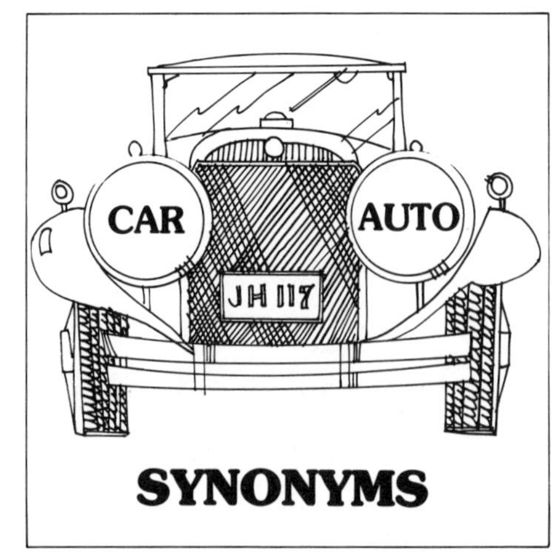

SYNONYMS

Synonyms are words that mean almost the same thing.

The words in Column I have synonyms in Column II. Can you match them? Copy both columns onto a separate sheet of paper. On your paper, put the letter from Column II in the blank in Column I.

Column I	Column II
______ 1. beautiful	a. liberty
______ 2. say	b. strike
______ 3. hit	c. sick
______ 4. tiny	d. alter
______ 5. change	e. risky
______ 6. lively	f. speak
______ 7. dangerous	g. pretty
______ 8. unhappy	h. small
______ 9. freedom	i. active
______ 10. ill	j. sad

Copy the following sentences onto a separate sheet of paper. Replace each underlined word with a synonym. You may use synonyms from the exercise you just finished.

1. I have a small dog.
2. My baby brother is ill.
3. Janet was very unhappy when her canary died.
4. It's risky to ride a bike at night without a light.
5. Do not hit a helpless person.
6. Say what you mean.
7. Alicia's dress for the prom was very beautiful.

ANTONYMS

Antonyms are words that mean the opposite.

The words in Column I have antonyms in Column II. Can you match them? Copy both columns onto a separate sheet of paper. On your paper, put the letter from Column II in the blank in Column I.

	Column I	Column II
______	1. old	a. before
______	2. short	b. lend
______	3. big	c. untidy
______	4. borrow	d. quiet
______	5. neat	e. long
______	6. end	f. little
______	7. noisy	g. fast
______	8. right	h. beginning
______	9. after	i. new
______	10. slowly	j. wrong

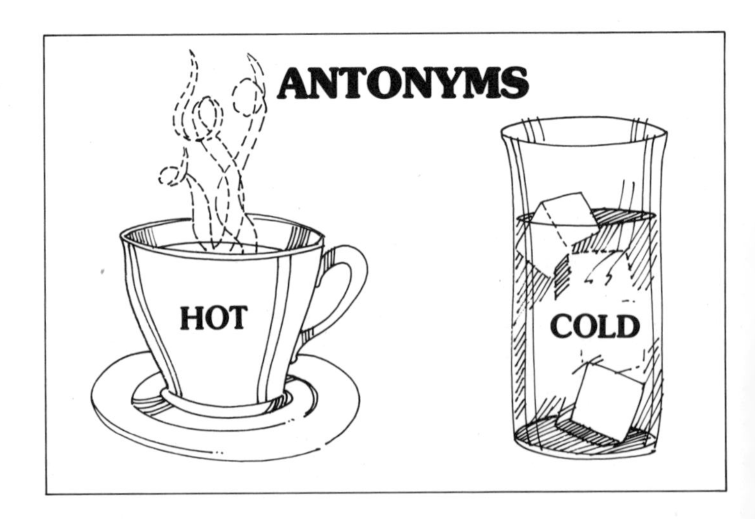

HOMONYMS

Homonyms are words that *sound alike.* They have different spellings and different meanings.

The words in Column I have homonyms in Column II. Can you match them? Copy both columns onto a separate sheet of paper. On your paper, put the letter from Column II in the blank in Column I.

	Column I	Column II
_____	1. see	a. piece
_____	2. peace	b. their
_____	3. raise	c. one
_____	4. write	d. way
_____	5. to, two	e. sea
_____	6. wood	f. right
_____	7. sew	g. would
_____	8. there	h. so
_____	9. weigh	i. too
_____	10. won	j. rays

Copy the following words onto a separate sheet of paper. Next to each word, write a homonym.

1. brake ________	5. seen ________
2. new ________	6. threw ________
3. hour ________	7. wait ________
4. hear ________	8. hole ________

Practice Using Homonyms

Copy the following sentences onto a separate sheet of paper. Underline the correct homonym for each sentence.

1. Michael ate the (whole, hole) pie by himself.
2. Looking down from the airplane, we saw the (scene, seen) of the city below.
3. The car's (breaks, brakes) did not work after they got wet.
4. David (new, knew) it was wrong to take money from his mother's purse.
5. Sixty minutes make one (our, hour).
6. Did you (hear, here) me call you?
7. Students come into the building (threw, through) the main door.
8. The (weight, wait) of the pack was heavy on Mark's shoulder.

More Practice Using Homonyms

Use each of the following homonyms in a sentence. There are ten pairs of homonyms, so you will have twenty sentences when you finish. Write your sentences on a separate sheet of paper.

seem	seam	fair	fare
heel	heal	road	rode
blue	blew	bare	bear
sail	sale	stair	stare
tail	tale	presents	presence

HETERONYMS

Heteronyms are words which are spelled the same, but can be pronounced two different ways. They also have two different meanings.

One example is the word object. An accent mark on the first syllable tells us one way to pronounce the word. (ob′ ject)

Alice found an *object* on the living room floor.

The accent mark on the second syllable changes the emphasis, the pronunciation, and the meaning of the word. (ob ject′)

Mother will *object* if you stay out too late.

Here are some other pairs of heteronyms. Use each word in a sentence. Write them on a separate sheet of paper. You should have ten sentences when you finish.

ref′ use	re fuse′	rec′ ord	re cord′
proj′ ect	pro ject′	prog′ ress	pro gress′
con′ duct	con duct′	con′ sole	con sole′

MULTIPLE MEANINGS

Our English language is very special because many words have more than one meaning. Often, we understand the meaning of a word by the way it is used in a sentence. Look at these sentences which all contain the word "match".

1. We watched the tennis **match** on television.
2. Jennifer struck a **match** to light the fire.
3. Joe's shirt did not **match** his pants.
4. Ken and Chris made a good **match**.
5. The pieces of the puzzle were difficult to **match**.
6. The basketball team was trying to **match** last year's winning record.

The following words have more than one meaning. On a separate sheet of paper, write at least two sentences for each word. Use a different meaning of the word in each sentence.

mass	bark	swing	hit	stand	hand

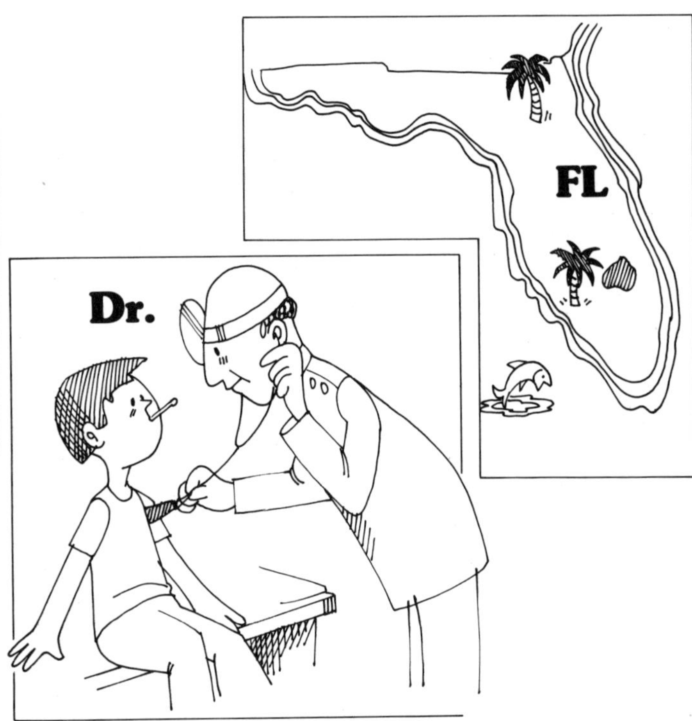

ABBREVIATIONS

Are you ever in a hurry? Sometimes, we can save time by making words shorter. When we write words in a shorter form, we abbreviate. Abbreviations are usually followed by a period, but not always. You will have to learn some exceptions in the lists of abbreviations that follow.

Group 1

Months of the Year

January	=	Jan.
February	=	Feb.
March	=	Mar.
April	=	Apr.
May	=	no abbreviations
June	=	no abbreviations
July	=	no abbreviations
August	=	Aug.
September	=	Sept.
October	=	Oct.
November	=	Nov.
December	=	Dec.

Group 2

Days of the Week

Sunday	=	Sun.
Monday	=	Mon.
Tuesday	=	Tues.
Wednesday	=	Wed.
Thursday	=	Thurs.
Friday	=	Fri.
Saturday	=	Sat.

Use abbreviations in the following sentences for all the months of the year and the days of the week. Write the sentences, with abbreviations, on a separate sheet of paper.

Remember—When an abbreviation comes at the end of a telling or commanding sentence, only one period is needed.

1. George's brother was born on Thursday, June 20, 1974.
2. Trees are prettiest in the autumn months of September and October.
3. Father will attend a meeting on Wednesday, June 26th.
4. The coldest months of the year are January, February, and March.
5. The rains in April help the flowers grow.
6. The school week is Monday, Tuesday, Wednesday, Thursday, and Friday.

Group 3—Addresses

Boulevard	=	Blvd.
Street	=	St.
Road	=	Rd.
Avenue	=	Ave.
Drive	=	Dr.
Court	=	Ct.
Place	=	Pl.
South	=	S.
East	=	E.
North	=	N.
West	=	W.

Group 4—Special Names

President	=	Pres.
Senator	=	Sen.
Representative	=	Rep.
Governor	=	Gov.
Doctor	=	Dr.
Reverend	=	Rev.
Mister	=	Mr.
Mistress	=	Mrs.
Mistress	=	Ms.
Colonel	=	Col.
Major	=	Maj.
Lieutenant	=	Lt.
Sergeant	=	Sgt.
Junior	=	Jr.
Senior	=	Sr.
Brothers	=	Bros.
Company	=	Co.
Corporation	=	Corp.

Use abbreviations in the following sentences for addresses and special names. Write the sentences, with abbreviations, on a separate sheet of paper.

1. Doctor Martha J. Smith moved her office from 8 South Michigan Avenue to 55 West Washington Street.
2. Representative John Render planned to run for Senator and then for President of the United States.
3. While in the Army, Chris Anderson was promoted from Lieutenant to Colonel.
4. Jerry Jenkins, Junior, went into partnership with his father, Jerry Jenkins, Senior.
5. Repairs are being made on Beacon Boulevard, Riley Road, Dillman Drive, Columbus Court, and Park Place.

Group 5
Measurements
(International Metric System)

millimeter	=	mm
centimeter	=	cm
meter	=	m
kilometer	=	km
milliliter	=	ml
centiliter	=	cl
litre	=	L
kilolitre	=	kl
milligram	=	mg
centigram	=	cg
gram	=	g
kilogram	=	kg
metric ton or tonne	=	t

Group 6
Measurements
(U.S. Customary System)

inch	=	in.
foot feet	=	ft.
yard	=	yd.
mile	=	mi.
pint	=	pt.
quart	=	qt.
gallon	=	gal.
ounce	=	oz.
pound	=	lb.
dozen	=	doz.

Group 7
Measurements (time)

minute	=	min.
hour	=	hr.
week	=	wk.
month	=	mo.
months	=	mos.
year	=	yr.

Group 8
Common Abbreviations

Parent Teacher Association	=	P.T.A.
Rural Routes; Railroad	=	R.R.
Registered Nurse	=	R.N.
Very Important Person	=	V.I.P.
Central Intelligence Agency	=	C.I.A.
Federal Bureau of Investigation	=	F.B.I.
Ante Meridian (12:00 midnight to 12:00 noon)	=	A.M.
Post Meridian (12:00 noon to 12:00 midnight)	=	P.M.
Cash on Delivery	=	C.O.D.
Television	=	TV
Extra Sensory Perception	=	E.S.P.
District Attorney	=	D.A.
Send Answer Please (from the French, repondez s'il vous plait)	=	R.S.V.P.
Tuberculosis	=	T.B.
Intelligence Quotient	=	I.Q.
Federal Housing Authority	=	F.H.A.
Veneral Disease	=	V.D.

Use these common abbreviations and the abbreviations for measurements in the following sentences. Write the sentences, with abbreviations, on a separate sheet of paper.

1. The letter from the Parent Teacher Association to Jane's mom, a Registered Nurse, said to "Repondez s'il vous plait."
2. It took one month for the package from Europe to arrive.
3. Jack grew twelve inches, or one foot, in a year, and he gained twenty pounds.
4. The package weighed three kilograms and was sent to Marge cash on delivery.
5. Alice used one pint of lemonade, one quart of orange sherbet, one gallon of ginger ale, and six cans of frozen orange juice to make the punch.
6. Bob's favorite television program was about the Federal Bureau of Investigation.
7. Jason's shopping list included the following items: one kilogram ground beef, one liter milk, and one meter red ribbon.
8. The distance from Amy's house to her school is 2.4 kilometers.

Group 8

Place Names

United States of America	= U.S.A.
United States	= U.S.
Mexico	= Mex.
Union of Soviet Socialist Republic (Russia)	= U.S.S.R.
West Germany	= W. Ger.

State Abbreviations

State	Traditional	Official Post Office
Alabama	Ala .	AL
Alaska	Alas.	AK
Arizona	Ariz.	AZ
Arkansas	Ark.	AR
California	Calif.	CA
Colorado	Colo.	CO
Connecticut	Conn.	CT
Delaware	Del.	DE
Florida	Fla.	FL
Georgia	Ga.	GA
Hawaii	none	HI
Idaho	Id., Ida.	ID
Illinois	Ill.	IL
Indiana	Ind.	IN
Iowa	Ia.	IA
Kansas	Kan., Kans.	KS
Kentucky	Ky.	KY
Louisiana	La.	LA
Maine	Me.	ME
Maryland	Md.	MD
Massachusetts	Mass.	MA
Michigan	Mich.	MI
Minnesota	Minn.	MN
Mississippi	Miss.	MS
Missouri	Mo.	MO
Montana	Mont.	MT
Nebraska	Neb., Nebr.	NE
Nevada	Nev.	NV
New Hampshire	N.H.	NH
New Jersey	N.J.	NJ
New Mexico	N. Mex.	NM
New York	N.Y.	NY
North Carolina	N.C.	NC
North Dakota	N. Dak.	ND
Ohio	O.	OH
Oklahoma	Okla.	OK
Oregon	Oreg.	OR
Pennsylvania	Pa., Penn.	PA
Rhode Island	R.I.	RI
South Carolina	S.C.	SC
South Dakota	S. Dak.	SD
Tennessee	Tenn.	TN
Texas	Tex.	TX
Utah	Ut.	UT
Vermont	Vt.	VT
Virginia	Va.	VA
Washington	Wash.	WA
West Virginia	W. Va.	WV
Wisconsin	Wis., Wisc.	WI
Wyoming	Wyo.	WY

Use abbreviations for the geographical locations in the following sentences. Write the sentences, with abbreviations, on a separate sheet of paper.

1. Skiing is very popular in Vermont, Colorado, and Wisconsin.
2. The forty-ninth and fiftieth states of the United States of America are Alaska and Hawaii.
3. Many television programs are broadcast from California and New York.
4. A popular resort city on the Atlantic Coast is Miami Beach, Florida.
5. The smallest state in the continental United States is Rhode Island, and the largest state is Texas.
6. Canada and Mexico are the two countries which border the United States of America.

CONTRACTIONS

Contractions are words which have been made shorter by leaving out letters. An apostrophe is used where the letter or letters have been left out.

Some words can be contracted or made shorter when they are written. International is often contracted to internat'l when written.

The most common contractions are those which combine two or more words into one shorter word. The new word has its own pronunciation. These contractions give variety to the English language. They offer another way to express your feelings. Can you hear a difference in these two sentences?

"I'll do it."

"I will do it."

On a separate sheet of paper, write the two words that make up the following contractions.

1. can't	5. I'm
2. won't	6. you'll
3. we're	7. you've
4. hasn't	8. they're

On a separate sheet of paper, write the contractions for the following words.

1. do not	6. did not	11. would not	16. let us
2. he is	7. it is	12. he will	17. there is
3. I have	8. does not	13. was not	18. are not
4. were not	9. you are	14. that is	19. will not
5. have not	10. they have	15. who is	20. should not

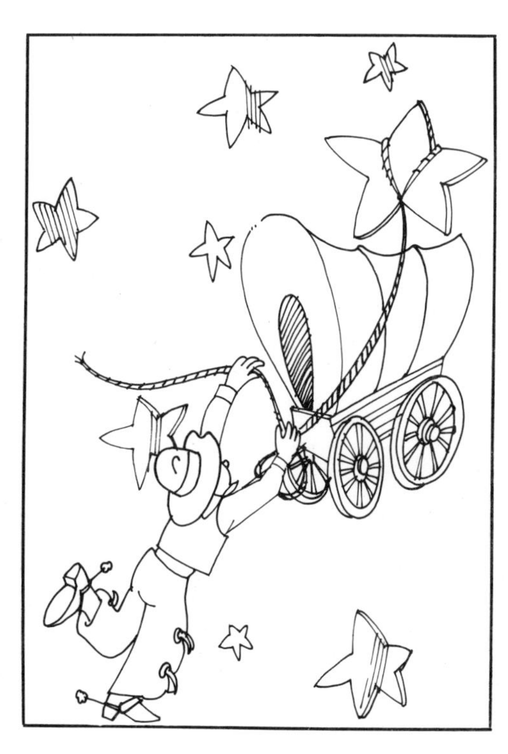

FAMILIAR SAYINGS

Sometimes, people like to use colorful words and expressions to communicate. Familiar sayings are a way to create a picture by using a few words and to communicate an unusual meaning. These sayings are also called proverbs.

Have you ever heard the expression, "Hitch your wagon to a star." What picture or image do you see? What message is this proverb trying to communicate?

People all over give the same meaning to proverbs and understand them to mean a specific thing. "Hitch your wagon to a star" means to make high goals for yourself, to aim high in life, to try for the best.

What do the following familiar sayings or proverbs mean to you?

1. To have a friend is to be a friend.
2. Birds of a feather flock together.
3. When it rains, it pours.
4. The grass is always greener on the other side.
5. Look before you leap.
6. Where there is smoke, there is fire.
7. The early bird catches the worm.
8. A stitch in time saves nine.

Which is the best explanation of the underlined sayings in each of the following stories? Write the numbers of the stories on a separate sheet of paper. Next to each number, write the letter of the explanation which you think is best.

1. "I earned three dollars cutting grass," said Joe. "At first I was going to buy a new record album, but then I decided to save it for a rainy day."

Joe planned to . . .

a. keep it till the next rainstorm.

b. purchase a raincoat.

c. save the money until he needs it for something very important.

2. "If you don't stop wasting your time in class," warned the teacher, "you'll be skating on thin ice as graduation time gets closer."

The teacher was saying . . .

a. "You'll have to skate near the edge of the rink."

b. "You'll be in danger of failing."

c. "You'll get ice skates for graduation."

3. "I can outplay anyone in school on the tennis court," boasted Ralph. "Even if you can," Fred replied, "don't blow your own horn."

Fred was saying . . .

a. "Don't brag about yourself."

b. "Don't sign up for band."

c. "Don't play your trumpet."

4. "James tore my paper," complained Harry to his teacher. "Well, don't tear his in return, or you'll just be adding fuel to the fire," Mr. Collins replied.

Mr. Collins was talking about . . .

a. making the books catch on fire.

b. making the problem bigger.

c. pouring gas onto the flames.

5. Sara's father was a famous baseball player. After Sara hit a homerun, her coach said, "Sara, You're a chip off the old block."

Sara's coach meant . . .

a. "You're better than your father."

b. "You have the same ability to play baseball as your father."

c. "Your appearance is the same as your father's."

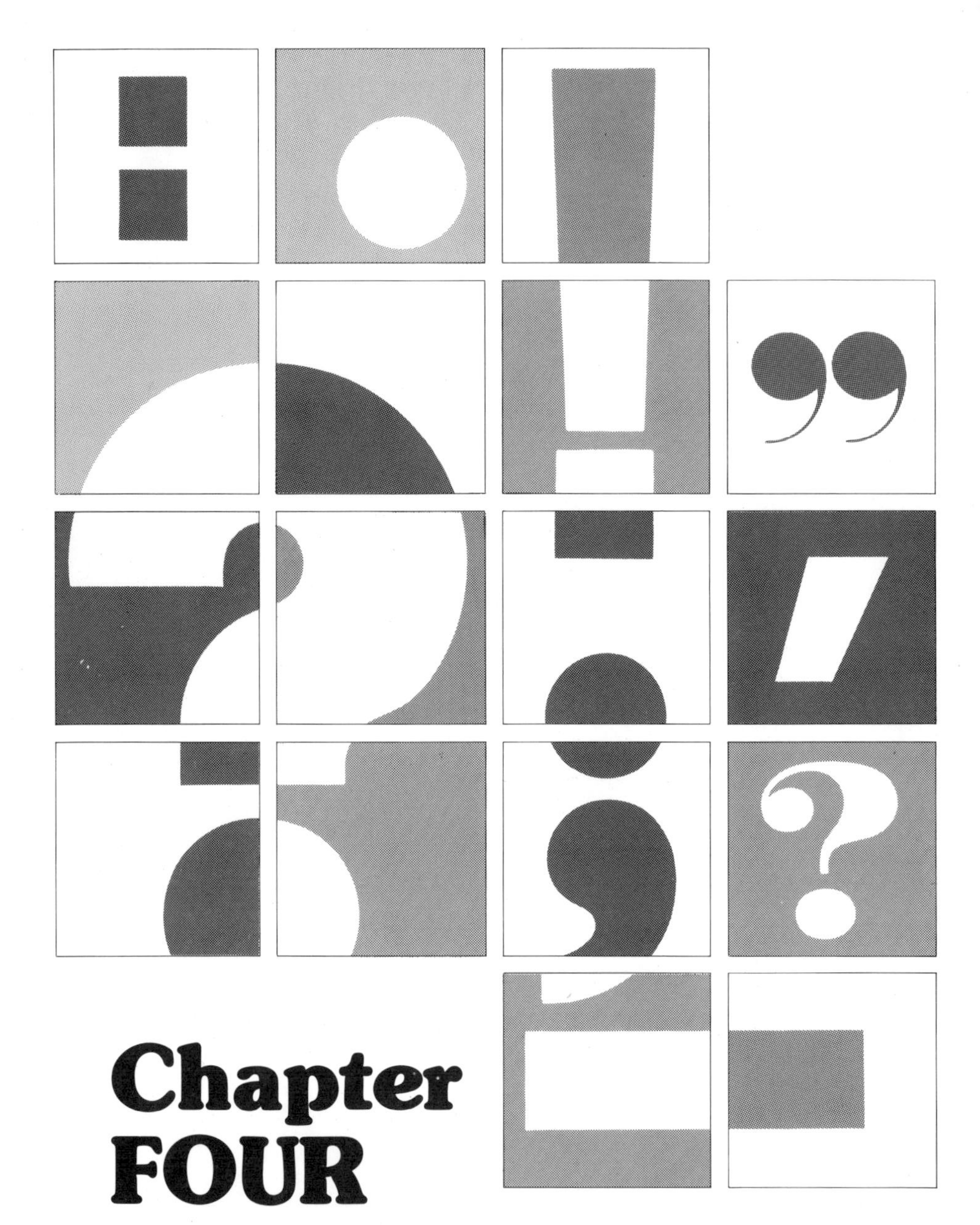

Chapter FOUR

DO I KNOW HOW TO USE THE PUNCTUATION MARKS?

When we speak, we help make our meaning clear by the use of our voices. We drop our voices and stop talking as a signal for the end of a sentence. We raise our voices as a signal for a question.

These voice signals cannot be used when we write. We must use other signals to make our meaning clear. Therefore, we use a period as a signal for the end of a sentence and a question mark as a signal for a question. You already know some of these punctuation marks.

END PUNCTUATION

USE A PERIOD (.)

1. *after a telling or commanding sentence.*
2. *after an initial.*
3. *after certain abbreviations.*

USE A QUESTION MARK (?)

after a sentence that asks a question.

USE AN EXCLAMATION POINT (!)

1. *after a sentence that shows strong feeling.*
2. *after a command that shows strong feeling.*

Copy the following sentences onto a separate sheet of paper. Then, place the proper punctuation marks where they belong.

1. Were you late to school this morning
2. I missed the bus and had to walk in the rain
3. Jim Dolan said that he has never been late for school in nine years
4. Don't stay up for the Late Show on Wednesday night
5. What an accomplishment to graduate with a perfect attendance record
6. Mr J D Hayes says that it is very important to be on time to class
7. Stop being late or you won't be a good job risk

COMMAS

USE A COMMA (,)

1. *to separate the name of the city and state.*

   Detroit, Michigan

2. *to separate the day of the month and year*

   July 4, 1976

3. *after the greeting of a friendly letter.*

   Dear Bill,

4. *after the closing of a letter.*

   Yours truly,

5. *to separate the items in a series.*

   grapes, apples, plums, and pears

6. *to set off words at the beginning of a sentence, such as* yes, no, well, oh

   Yes, bees make honey.
   No, ice does not sink.

7. *to set off names when talking to someone.*

   Ms. Thompson, may I introduce my mother?

8. *before the joining words* and, but, or, nor *in a compound sentence.*

   Curt can bring the potato chips for
   the party, and Sally will make the popcorn.

9. *after an introductory clause which cannot stand alone in a sentence.*

   Although cigarette smoking is dangerous
   to your health, many people still start smoking.

Copy the following sentences onto a separate sheet of paper and put in commas where they belong.

NIAGARA FALLS

1. Yes Niagara Falls is a wonderful place to visit.
2. When we were there beautiful colored lights fell upon the rushing water.
3. One side of the Falls is the American Falls which belong to the United States and the other side is the Horseshoe Falls which belong to Canada.
4. The American side is in Niagara Falls New York.
5. From the American Falls a visitor can take a thirty-minute miniature train ride which stops at Cave of the Winds Three Sisters Islands Great Island and other points along the Falls.
6. With a tremendous rush of water the Falls crash 182 feet to the river below.
7. In 1929 Canada signed an agreement to protect the beauty of the Falls.
8.

8570 Snow Road
Cleveland Ohio
August 15 1975

Dear Mom

We are at the Falls and they are beautiful. We'll be home soon.

Your son
Bill

APOSTROPHES

USE AN APOSTROPHE (')

1. *in a contraction to show that a letter or letters have been left out.*

   do not = don't   will not = won't   could not = couldn't

2. *in a possessive to show ownership.*

   a. Mary owns a record player. To show her ownership, we say, "Mary's record player". Notice that the apostrophe goes in front of the *s*.

   b. The children have some toys. To show this ownership, we say, "the children's toys". Notice again that the apostrophe is in front of the *s*.

   c. The boys have bicycles. To show this ownership, we say, "the boys' bicycles". Notice that the apostrophe goes *after* the s because there are several boys.

Remember—
- *If the word that shows ownership does not end in* s, *we add two things–an apostrophe and an* s.
- *If the word that shows ownership ends in* s, *we add only one thing–an apostrophe.*

Practice Using Apostrophes

Copy the following sentences onto a separate sheet of paper, and put in the **'s** or the **'** only to show ownership.

1. The family __ vacation was spent at the National Park.
2. The campground __ rules warned people not to get too close to the bears.
3. Tuesday __ biggest event was the children __ excitement when they saw the bear tracks.
4. Some people try to get the bears close enough for their camera __ view.
5. It would be fun to show the bear __ pictures at school when they returned.

6. The bears __ hunger will draw them close to cars or people where there might be food.
7. Some people __ carelessness in leaving food or garbage attracts the bears __ attention.
8. A dog __ bark will also bring a bear out of the woods.
9. A bear __ huge paws can rip open a car __ convertible top.
10. The car __ windows should not be rolled down more than a few inches for the visitor __ safety.

YELLOWSTONE NATIONAL PARK

More Practice Using Apostrophes

Copy the following phrases onto a separate sheet of paper, and put an **'s** or just the **'** in each blank.

1. children __ toys
2. Father __ car
3. boys __ jackets
4. the football team __ score
5. Alice __ money
6. my friend __ parents
7. the dog __ food
8. her brother __ job
9. all the books __ covers
10. the ladies __ hats

QUOTATION MARKS

USE QUOTATION MARKS (" ")

to show the exact words of a speaker.

Ms. Smith said, "Bring your homework to my desk."

Notice that only Ms. Smith's words are enclosed in quotation marks, and that a comma is used to separate her exact words from the rest of the sentence.

The sentence can also be stated another way.

"Bring your homework to my desk," Ms. Smith said.

Notice again that her exact words are enclosed in quotation marks and separated from the rest of the sentence by a comma.

Copy the following sentences onto a separate sheet of paper. Put quotation marks around the exact words of the person speaking. Also, remember to separate the quotation from the rest of the sentence with a comma.

1. You're late for school again said Mrs. Davis.
2. Our bus was late this morning answered Barry.
3. Mrs. Davis replied You'll have to get a pass from the office.
4. I just came from the office, and they will make the announcement over the intercom Barry explained.
5. Here's the announcement now stated Mrs. Davis.
6. Mrs. Davis told the class Let's listen.
7. Please admit to class students from Bus 11 announced the principal.
8. Jean spoke up Our bus was late yesterday.
9. I hope our bus is late tomorrow Fred added.
10. It gets very cold while you wait for the bus Barry answered.

COLONS

USE A COLON (:)

1. *after the greeting of a business letter.*

Dear Ms. Jones:

2. *when writing time.*

10:35

HYPHENS

USE A HYPHEN (-)

to divide syllables of a broken word.

Sometimes, when writing or typing, there isn't enough room on a line to finish a word. Divide the word at a syllable ending, and put a hyphen to show the word is continued on the next line.

UNDERLINING

USE UNDERLINING (____________)

for the titles of books, magazines, and newspapers.

<u>The Daily News</u>

<u>Scholastic Magazine</u>

<u>A Hobby Book for Building Model Cars</u>

Practice Using Colons, Hyphens, and Underlining

Copy the following sentences onto a separate sheet of paper. Put in colons, hyphens, and underlining where they are needed.

1. Izvestia is the name of Russia's official newspaper.
2. "Dear Sir or Madam" is a good greeting for a business letter.
3. Jaws, by Peter Benchley, is an exciting and scary book.
4. Helen works every day from 4 00 to 7 30.
5. Hyphens are used to divide words into syllables, as math ematics.

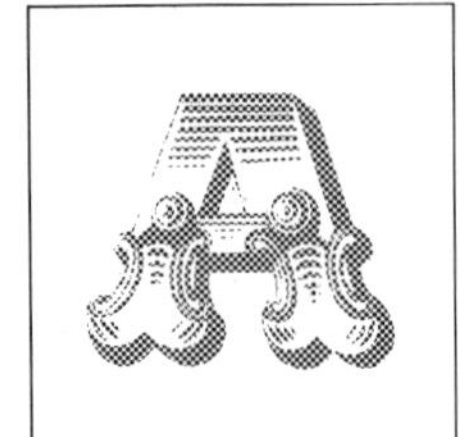

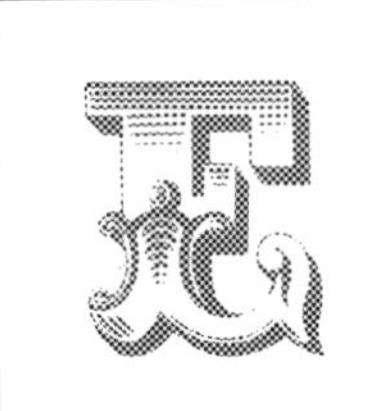
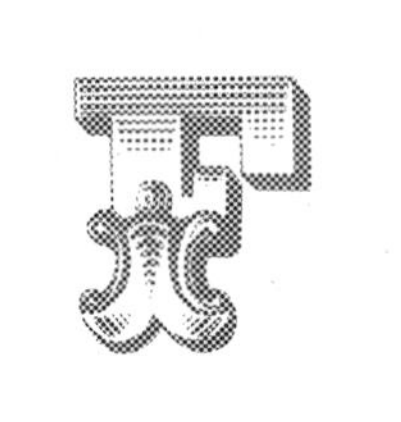

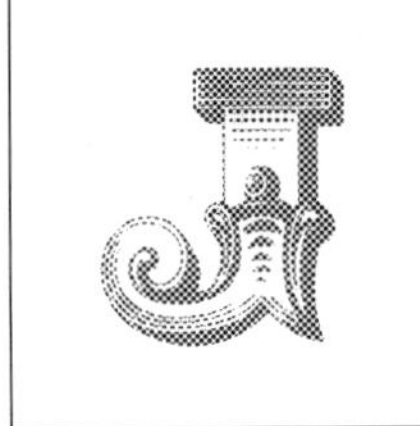

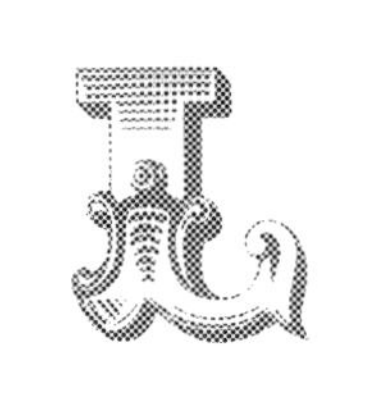

Chapter FIVE

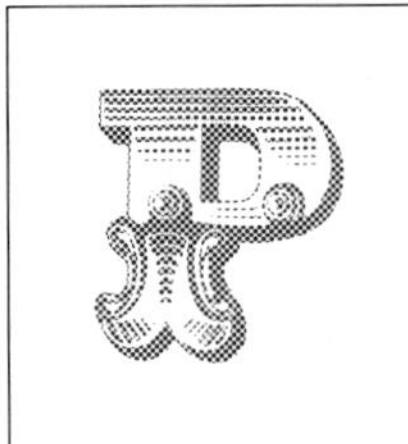
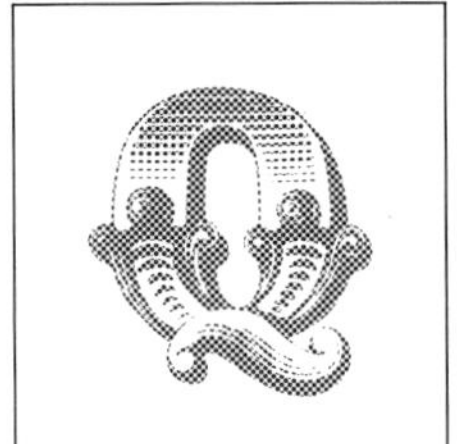

WHEN DO I USE CAPITAL LETTERS?

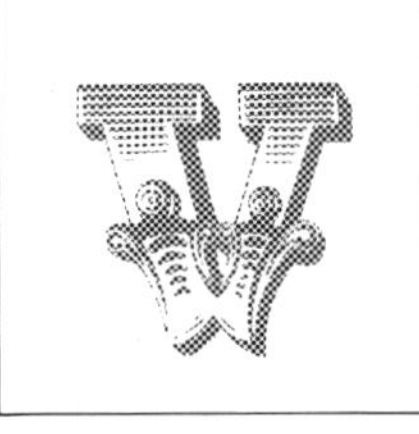
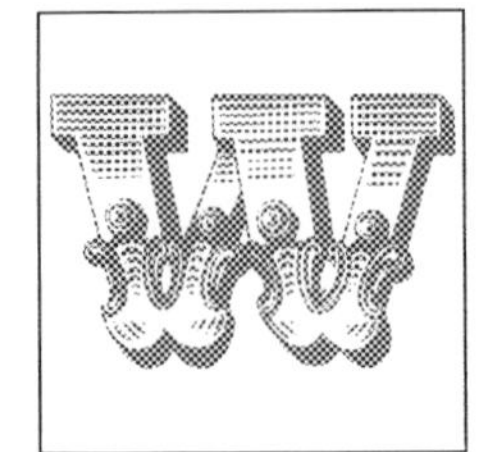

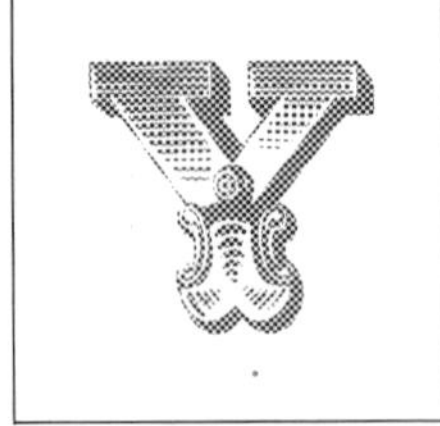

USING CAPITAL LETTERS

Capital letters are signals used both in reading and writing. They quickly catch our eye because they are larger than the other letters on a page. Capital letters are used at the beginning of words to tell us many things. The following rules help us to know when to use capital letters.

Capital letters are used to show:

Rule 1. *The first word of a sentence*

Football games are fun to watch.

Rule 2. *Names of persons and names of pets*

Mary Jane Rogers, Rover

Rule 3. *Names such as Father or Mother when they are used as a person's name*

I missed the bus, Mother.

Names such as aunt, uncle, or cousin when they are used with a name

Uncle George, Aunt Mary

Practice Using Rules 1, 2, and 3

Copy the following sentences onto a separate sheet of paper. Put in capital letters where they belong. Check with rules 1, 2, and 3.

a. vacation time gives us a chance to visit new places.

b. last July, mother and dad took our family to Washington, D.C. to see our government at work.

c. we had to leave our dog, snoopy, with uncle fred and aunt mary.

d. our neighbor, dennis lange, told us to be sure to visit the President's home.

e. my cousin mario told us to see the Tomb of the Unknown Soldier.

Capital letters are also used to show:

Rule 4. *Names of the days of the week*
Monday, Wednesday
Names of months of the year
January, July
Names of holidays
Christmas, Easter

Rule 5. *Names of cities*
Chicago, Los Angeles
Names of states
Illinois, California

Rule 6. *Names of countries*
United States, France
Names of continents
Africa, Asia

Practice Using Rules 4, 5, and 6

Copy the following sentences onto a separate sheet of paper. Put in the capital letters where they belong. Check with rules 4, 5, and 6.

a. We left on our vacation on saturday morning.

b. Father drove through several states, including pennsylvania and virginia.

c. We arrived in washington, d.c., the capital of the u.s.a., on july 3.

d. The next day, july 4, was independence day.

e. Driving down the street, we saw flags from england, russia, and japan.

THE WHITE HOUSE

Capital letters are used to show more things:

Rule 7. *Names of nationalities; that is, the names of groups of people from different countries.*

Italian, French, Spanish, American, Chinese

Names of languages spoken by people of different countries.

German, Russian, Swedish

Rule 8. *Names of streets, avenues, roads, and rural routes*

Pine Street, Michigan Avenue, Hillcrest Road, R.R. 1

Rule 9. *Names of business companies and buildings.*

Standard Oil Company, John Hancock Building

Practice Using Rules 7, 8, and 9

Copy the following sentences onto a separate sheet of paper. Put in the capital letters where they belong. Check with rules 7, 8, and 9.

a. We saw german, irish, polish and greek people celebrating with the americans.

b. The people who make our laws meet in the capitol building.

c. The President lives in the white house, which is on pennsylvania avenue.

d. We were surprised to learn that the white house has 132 rooms.

e. We bought some post cards of Washington, D.C. at the walgreen drug store.

THE CAPITOL BUILDING

Capital letters are used to show:

Rule 10. *Names of rivers, oceans, and mountains*
Mississippi River, Pacific Ocean, Smoky Mountains

Rule 11. *Names of churches and religions*
First Presbyterian Church, Moslem, Christianity

Rule 12. *The word God and all words that refer to God*

Rule 13. *Names of clubs and organizations*
Lions Club, Red Cross

Practice Using Rules 10, 11, 12, and 13

Copy the following sentences onto a separate sheet of paper. Put in the capital letters where they belong. Check with rules 10, 11, 12, and 13.

a. The Lincoln Memorial is located on the banks of the potomac river.

b. A beautiful 105 mile road winds through the blue ridge mountains near Washington, D.C.

c. The atlantic ocean is not far from our nation's capital.

d. Many presidents and their families have attended st. john's episcopal church.

e. The american historical association is also located in Washington, D.C.

THE LINCOLN MEMORIAL

More capital letters are used to show:

Rule 14. *Some abbreviations*

P.O. (Post Office), R.R. (Rural Route), and C.O.D. (Cash on Delivery)

Rule 15. *Titles of persons*

Miss, Mr., Mrs., Dr., Ms.

Rule 16. *Initials*

J.D.

Practice Using Rules 14, 15, and 16.

Copy the following sentences onto a separate sheet of paper. Put in the capital letters where they belong. Check with rules 14, 15, and 16.

a. Our tour guide, mr. h. smith, took us to the Bureau of Engraving and Printing where the government prints paper money.

b. It would be nice to touch so much money, but mr. smith explained that visitors can only watch from the platform.

c. Another guide, mrs. r.b. king, explained that a dollar bill wears out within fifteen months, and that new money must be printed to replace it.

d. Also, mrs. king told us that paper money is counted twelve times by different people and machines to make sure that none of it disappears.

e. Before the end of the tour, mrs. king added that the Bureau also prints postage stamps and invitations to White House affairs.

PRINTING PAPER MONEY

Capital letters are used to show:

Rule 17. *Names of railroads, airlines, bus lines, and ships*

Illinois Central Railroad, American Airlines, Greyhound Bus, S.S. France

Rule 18. *Names of historical events and documents*

Civil War, the Constitution of the United States

Rule 19. *Names of departments of government*

Department of Justice

Practice Using Rules 17, 18 and 19.

Copy the following sentences onto a separate sheet of paper. Put in the capital letters where they belong. Check rules 17, 18 and 19.

a. Many people arrive in Washington, D.C. by greyhound bus, amtrack, and united airlines.

b. The declaration of independence was signed on July 4, 1776.

c. The department of health, education, and welfare gives a Social Security number to every citizen who works.

d. We toured the offices of the federal bureau of investigation, which is called the F.B.I., while visiting the department of justice.

e. Guards protect the declaration of independence, the constitution, and the bill of rights, which are kept in glass cases during the day. At night, these documents are lowered into a bombproof, fireproof safe.

Capital letters are used to show:

Rule 20. *First word in each line of poetry*

"Help." she cried. "My fish has died.
The cat was quicker than the fish.
And now there is an empty dish!"

Rule 21. *First word in the closing of a letter*

Your friend,

Rule 22. *The word I*

She and I are friends.

Practice Using Rules 20, 21, and 22.

Copy the following sentences onto a separate sheet of paper. Put in the capital letters where they belong. Check with rules 20, 21, and 22.

a. In the middle of the trip, i sent Cousin Mario a postcard.

b. Here is the short poem i decided to write on the postcard.

c. yes, i miss you, Mario, my friend.
but soon my vacation will come to an end.
for you a nice souvenir i chose.
and now my poem will have to close.

d. I signed it—your pal,
Joe

e. I hope he receives my postcard before i get home.

Finally, capital letters are used to show:

Rule 23. *First, last, and all important words in titles of books, stories, songs, poems, magazines, and newspapers*

Murder on the Orient Express
"Sounds of Silence"
Field and Stream

Rule 24. *In written conversation, the first word of a speaker*

Sharon said, "It is a lovely day."

Practice Using Rules 23 and 24.

Copy the following sentences onto a separate sheet of paper. Put in the capital letters where they belong. Check with rules 23 and 24.

a. We were able to see so many more things on our vacation because we bought the book, visitor's guide of washington.

b. On our way home, Mother told Dad, "i am glad our neighbor told us about that book."

c. When we pulled into our driveway, Mario came running and shouting, "welcome home!"

d. Mother said, "it was a great vacation."

e. I told Mario, "there are so many things to tell you."

Chapter SIX

DO I UNDERSTAND HOW TO USE MY LANGUAGE?

VERBS

ACTION VERBS

When we express ourselves, we talk about people and things. We also need to tell what the people and things are doing. Verbs are words that tell about actions.

Examples: The pie **burned**.

A car **crashed**.

The bell **rang**.

Carl **ran**.

They **laughed**.

Our team **won**.

What are the action words in these sentences? Copy the numbers 1 to 10 on a separate sheet of paper. After each number, write the verb for the sentence.

1. Many people ride bicycles in the fall.
2. Some people rake leaves from their lawns.
3. Gardeners plant seeds for early spring flowers.
4. Winter brings cold weather.
5. People shovel lots of snow.
6. My friends ice-skate at the park.
7. Rain comes in the spring.
8. Baseball teams practice for the season.
9. Our family buys new clothes for Easter.
10. My cousins fish during the summer.

VERB PHRASES

The words **am, is, was,** and **were** do not show action, but they are verbs, too.

Examples: John **is** in the cafeteria.

The girls **are** here.

I **am** in high school.

Mary **was** home yesterday.

The records **were** in the cabinet.

Sometimes verbs need helpers. Then the verb and the helper act as the *verb phrase.*

The following verbs are used as helpers and as main verbs:

has, have, had

is, are, was, were

do, does, did

could, can, would, should

will, shall, might

Number a separate sheet of paper from 1 to 10, and copy the verb phrases in each of the following sentences.

1. Many people are watching television programs about hospitals and medicine.
2. As a result of these programs, interest in health has increased.
3. People can learn about health by watching medical programs.
4. Medical information is checked carefully for each program.
5. Special programs have reported on health problems which could happen to anyone.
6. Some medical programs do use rare diseases and their effects on people for the subject of their shows.

7. A hospital does try to save every life possible.
8. Hospital programs do show the value of human life.
9. Medical programs have explained many careers in hospitals.
10. These programs may interest people in hospital jobs.

VERBS IN QUESTIONS

In sentences which ask questions, it is more difficult to pick out verb phrases. First, change the question to a telling sentence. Then, pick out the verb phrase.

Example: Are you going? Change to: You are going.
The verb phrase is are going.

On a separate sheet of paper, change the following questions to telling sentences. Then, underline the verb phrase in each.

1. Do you like music?
2. Have you sung in the school chorus?
3. Could you play an instrument in the band?
4. Can the students in your class read music?
5. Has rock music become your favorite?
6. How much money do you spend on records?
7. Would you go to a rock concert?
8. Have you attended a jazz concert?
9. Are you learning the new dances?
10. Do the band and chorus in your school have an annual concert?

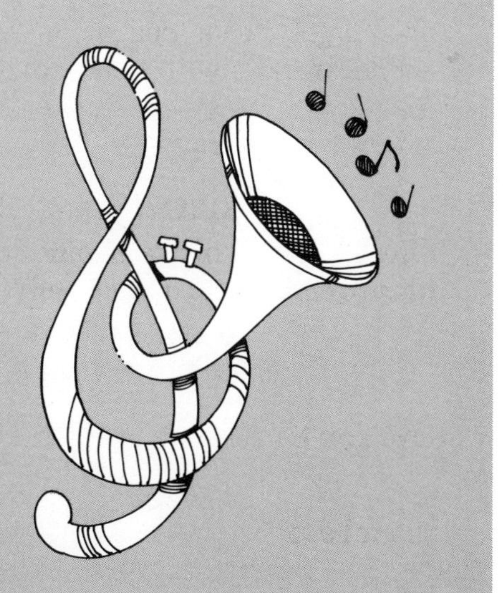

PRINCIPAL PARTS OF VERBS

Every verb has three main forms. They are called the **present, past,** and **past participle.** These are the three forms of the verb to eat:

Present	eat
Past	ate
Past participle	has eaten have eaten had eaten

Notice—The past participle of a verb must use either **has, have,** *or* **had** *as its helper.*

This is a list of the principal parts of some verbs which are used frequently. Remember that *has, have,* or *had* must be used with the past participle.

Present	Past	Past participle
ring	rang	rung
break	broke	broken
see	saw	seen
talk	talked	talked
run	ran	run
fall	fell	fallen
hear	heard	heard
teach	taught	taught
bring	brought	brought
ride	rode	ridden
drink	drank	drunk
write	wrote	written
freeze	froze	frozen
give	gave	given
learn	learned	learned

Present	Past	Past participle
go	went	gone
buy	bought	bought
take	took	taken
drive	drove	driven
speak	spoke	spoken
leave	left	left

On a separate sheet of paper, write these ten sentences. Choose either the past or past participle of the verbs in the parentheses. Remember, when you use a helper, you must use the past participle. Check with the list above.

1. When the noon bell (ring), Jeanette (leave) school for her vocational training job.
2. Her friend has (drive) her to work all semester.
3. Jeanette has always (take) her lunch to school and eats it on the way to work.
4. On the way, Jeanette and Paul talk about what they have (see) on TV the night before.
5. Each day, Jeanette has (bring) some of her father's tools to use at work.
6. She has not (break) any of them, because she has (learn) to handle them carefully.
7. She (hear) about a sale at the hardware store and she (buy) a tool box.
8. Her employer has (speak) to her about her work and has (write) a good report to Jeanette's school.
9. On the job, her employer has (teach) her many things and has (give) Jeanette many responsibilities.
10. Jeanette enjoys the work and sometimes she has (go) there on Saturdays.

VERB TENSES

All verbs have tense. Tense means time. The three tenses of verbs are **present, past,** and **future.** Each of these sentences use one of the three tenses of the verb *to eat:*

Present	Larry eats his lunch.
Past	Larry ate his lunch.
Future	Larry will eat his lunch.

Things that happen now are in the **present tense.** Things that have already happened are in the **past tense.** Things that are going to happen are in the **future tense.**

Present	Today Mike and his friends see the school bus.
Past	They saw the same bus near their house yesterday.
Future	Tomorrow they will see it again.

When does the action take place in the following sentences? Can you tell the tense (time) of each verb? On a separate sheet of paper, number from 1 to 10. Write present, past, or future for each verb.

1. Plants use light from the sun to make their food and to help them grow.
2. For thousands of years, plants have made their food from sunlight, water, and minerals in the soil.
3. There are more than 350,000 kinds of plants.
4. The subject of plant study was named botany.
5. Will you study botany in high school?
6. People buy many plants for their homes.

7. Green plants will make a room look good.
8. Plants store water in the roots, stems, and leaves.
9. I watered all my plants last night.
10. In spring, you will see plants in the forms of flowers, trees, and shrubs.

NOUNS

COMMON NOUNS

Words in our language that name persons, places, or things are called nouns.

In the sentences that follow, see if you can pick out the words that name persons, places, and things. The number of nouns in each sentence is in the margin. Number a separate sheet of paper from 1 to 10. Write the nouns for each sentence.

(2) 1. The government must protect its citizens.

(2) 2. Police help catch criminals.

(3) 3. The courts punish people who break the law.

(2) 4. A police officer can make an arrest.

(3) 5. Citizens can arrest a criminal if they see the crime happen.

(4) 6. A police officer should have a court order called a warrant before searching a home.

(6) 7. Anyone who is accused of a serious crime goes to jail until the court gives the person a trial.

(4) 8. People don't have to stay in jail if they pay enough money, called bail.

(4) 9. Bail is paid to make sure the accused person doesn't run away before having a trial in court.

(3) 10. It is the duty of a good citizen to obey the laws.

PROPER NOUNS

Some nouns are written with capital letters and some are written with small letters. A noun which gives the name of a particular person, place, or thing is called a proper noun. It is written with a capital letter. The nouns written with small letters are called common nouns.

Examples:

	Common Nouns	**Proper Nouns**
(person)	boy, girl	Carl, Mary
(place)	city	Milwaukee
(thing)	court	Supreme Court

Remember—*Use a capital letter when the noun names a particular or special person, place, or thing.*

SINGULAR AND PLURAL NOUNS

If a noun names one person, one place, or one thing, it is singular. Singular means one. If the noun names more than one person, place or thing, it is plural. Plural means more than one. *Usually an* **s** *is added to the end of a noun to make it plural.*

Examples:

Singular	**Plural**
book	book**s**
car	car**s**
school	school**s**
home	home**s**
friend	friend**s**
boy	boy**s**
girl	girl**s**
mother	mother**s**
father	father**s**
idea	idea**s**

Nouns which end in **s, sh, ch,** and **x,** *form their plurals by adding* **es.**

Examples:

Singular	Plural
dress	dresses
bush	bushes
church	churches
box	boxes
lunch	lunches
coach	coaches
guess	guesses
tax	taxes
watch	watches
peach	peaches

Nouns ending in **y** *with a consonant right before the* **y** *form their plurals by changing the* **y** *to* **i** *and adding* **es.**

Examples:

Singular	Plural
lady	ladies
family	families
candy	candies
story	stories
party	parties
sky	skies
copy	copies
baby	babies
library	libraries
city	cities

There are some nouns which form plurals differently than other nouns. There are no rules to follow for these nouns. Learn the plural forms.

Examples:

Singular	Plural
child	children
mouse	mice
tooth	teeth
woman	women
foot	feet
man	men
ox	oxen
goose	geese
sheep	sheep

Practice Using Plural Nouns

On a separate sheet of paper, write the plural of each of the following nouns:

Singular	Plural	Singular	Plural
1. foot		11. car	
2. baby		12. coach	
3. tax		13. mouse	
4. book		14. sky	
5. lunch		15. idea	
6. city		16. bush	
7. friend		17. ox	
8. school		18. party	
9. tooth		19. watch	
10. family		20. goose	

More Practice Using Plural Nouns

On a separate sheet of paper, copy the following paragraph and make plurals out of all the singular nouns that are in parentheses ().

It is a big job to keep a home happy and clean. (Man) and (woman) must learn many (skill). (Mother) and (father) help their (child) learn how to handle adult (responsibility). (School) also teach courses to help young people learn how to manage a home. Cooking, sewing, managing money, and care of (child) are important everyday skills. These (course) can help you, if you live by yourself or have a family.

SINGULAR POSSESSIVES

Nouns can show ownership. In writing, show ownership by using an apostrophe.

Examples:

Jim**'s** car
Joan**'s** notebook
A student**'s** lunch

To make a singular noun show ownership, add **'s**.

Use a separate sheet of paper, and show ownership by adding 's to the nouns in the phrases shown at the right.

1. (Mary) ring
2. (dog) bark
3. (sailor) hat
4. (farmer) horse
5. (Wayne) brother
6. (cousin) coat
7. (woman) child
8. (principal) office
9. (Ms. Hall) job
10. (book) title

PLURAL POSSESSIVES

Now, look at these plural nouns which show possession.

Examples:

boy**s'** games
neighbor**s'** houses
store**s'** windows

Plural nouns ending in **s**, *form their ownership by adding only the ' to the end of the word.*

Use a separate sheet of paper and show ownership by adding only an ' to the noun in each of the phrases shown at the right.

1. (girls) jackets
2. (teachers) room
3. (stores) sales
4. (cars) licenses
5. (trees) leaves
6. (horses) saddles
7. (hunters) dogs
8. (babies) toys
9. (Indians) tents
10. (flags) colors

MORE PLURAL POSSESSIVES

Finally, there are some nouns which are plural, but do not end in s.

Examples:

children's bikes

women's jobs

Plural nouns not ending in **s** *form their ownership by adding the* **'s**.

Use a separate sheet of paper. Show ownership by adding the 's to the nouns in the phrases shown at the right.

1. (men) golf clubs
2. (women) locker rooms
3. (oxen) tails
4. (teeth) cavities
5. (people) notes
6. (geese) feathers
7. (deer) antlers

PRONOUNS

Pronouns are words that are used instead of nouns.

Examples:

Mary went to the store.	**She** went to the store.
Dave gave Mike the money.	Dave gave **him** the money.
Phil lost Phil's pencil.	Phil lost **his** pencil.
The bread is fresh.	**It** is fresh.

Here are some common pronouns. The groups tell what the pronouns do.

I **Do the Action**	I, we, you he, she, it, they
II **Receive the Action**	me, you, it her, him, us, them
III **Show Ownership**	my, mine our, ours, its your, yours, his, her, hers
IV **Point Out**	this, these, that, those

Write the following sentences on a separate sheet of paper. Choose the correct pronoun for each sentence.

Use pronouns from Section I for these sentences:

1. Pat and (I, me) study together.
2. (Him, He) and his friend worked on the car.
3. (They, Them) ate in the cafeteria.
4. (Us, We) went to the dance.
5. (She, Her) and I are friends.

Use pronouns from Section II for these sentences:

1. Carol gave (me, I) a birthday present.
2. Richard saw (him, he) leave the building.
3. Chris brought (we, us) some potato chips.
4. I gave (they, them) the picture.
5. Did you help (her, she)?

Use pronouns from Section III for these sentences:
Remember—*Never use an apostrophe to show ownership with pronouns.*

1. That dog is (our's, ours).
2. (There, Their) pets sleep in the basement.
3. Is that bird (yours, your's)?
4. The hamster is (her's, hers).
5. Where is (you're, your) dog kept?

Use pronouns from Section IV for these sentences:
Remember—1. *The words this and that are singular.*
2. *The words these and those are plural.*

1. (This, These) pen is mine.
2. (This, These) pens are mine.
3. (That, Those) book is John's.
4. (That, Those) books are John's.

Practice Using Pronouns

Number a separate sheet of paper from 1 to 10. Write the ten pronouns you find in the following paragraph.

Many people like to wear jewelry. Our ideas about jewelry are often very different. Rings, earrings, bracelets, and necklaces can make an outfit look good. These pieces of jewelry can be made of different materials. They can be cheap or very expensive. Some women have their ears pierced. They feel pretty when they wear earrings. Some men wear bracelets, rings, and chains. Their bracelets might be made of metal, leather, or wood. You might like necklaces made of shells. Some people will notice you if you wear attractive jewelry.

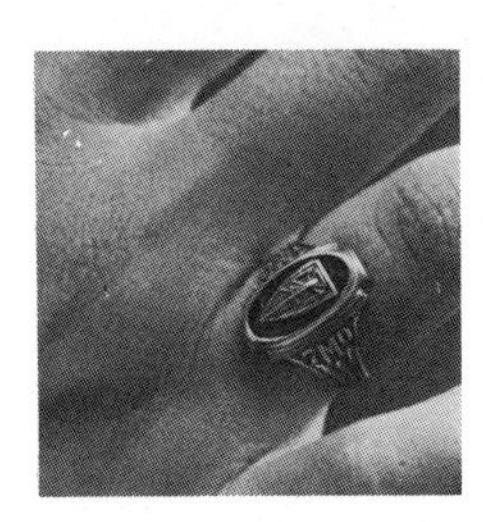

More Practice Using Pronouns

Copy the following sentences onto a separate sheet of paper and use a pronoun from the following list for each underlined word.

we	**her**
she	**they**
he	**them**
you	**their**
its	**him**
his	**us**

1. Many kids like tennis, and kids play a lot during the summer.
2. Tanya says that Tanya's mother is a good tennis player.
3. Tanya's friend Debbie says that Debbie likes to play softball.
4. Debbie plays on a softball team, and Debbie's position is pitcher.
5. The players have shirts with the team's name on the shirts.
6. The best birthday present for Debbie is to take Debbie to a Cubs game.
7. Bob likes to play basketball, and Bob is on the team.
8. The park provides people with a place to play basketball.
9. Basketball fans are happy that basketball fans can watch games on TV.
10. All basketball fans find a game between the Bucks and the Warriors exciting to basketball fans.

COMPARISON METHODS

WORDS THAT DESCRIBE

Words that describe change their forms when they are used to compare. Look at these examples:

I think cake tastes good. (describes one thing)

I like ice cream better. (compares two things—cake and ice cream)

I like a hot fudge sundae best. (compares more than two things—cake, ice cream, and a hot fudge sundae.)

Learn to use these words when you . . .

Describe things	Compare two things	Compare more than two things
bad	worse	worst
many	more	most
good	better	best

Copy the following sentences onto a separate sheet of paper. Fill in the blanks, choosing the correct word from the list above for each blank.

1. This history test is ______________.
2. The last test was even ______________.
3. The English test was the ______________ test of all.
4. There were ______________ people at last night's basketball game.
5. There will be ______________ people at the tournament games next week.
6. For the state championship game, there will be the ______________ people of all.
7. Country music is ______________.
8. I think rock music is ______________.
9. Classical music is the ______________ music of all.

More Words That Describe

Here is another group of words to use when you compare.

Describe things	Compare two things	Compare more than two things
long	longer	longest
tall	taller	tallest
hard	harder	hardest
small	smaller	smallest

Copy the following sentences onto a separate sheet of paper. Fill in the blanks, choosing the correct word from the list above for each blank.

1. Debbie, who is six feet, is a ______ girl.
2. Her friend Carol is one inch ______ than Debbie.
3. Lanette, who stands above her two friends, is the ______.
4. Paul ordered a ______ coke.
5. It was ______ than he wanted.
6. It was the ______ coke he had ever seen.
7. Some students think English is ______ to learn.
8. Some think that learning history is even ______.
9. ______ of all for some students is chemistry.
10. The math lesson was ______ yesterday.
11. The book for English class is even ______.
12. The report for history was the ______ assignment of all.

More Words that Compare

This last group of words is used to compare concepts or phrases rather than single words. The word **more** is used to compare two things, and the word **most** is used to compare more than two things.

Describes things	Compares two things	Compares more than two things
wonderful	more wonderful	most wonderful
expensive	more expensive	most expensive
careful	more careful	most careful

Copy the following sentences onto a separate sheet of paper. Fill in the blanks, choosing the correct word from the list above for each blank.

1. People should be ____________ when they ride their bikes.
2. They must be even ____________ when they learn to drive a car.
3. They should be the ________________ of all when they see children playing.
4. As a child, getting a puppy was a ____________________ experience for Tara.
5. As a teen-ager, learning to drive was even ____________.
6. Getting her own apartment, as a young adult, was the ____________________________ experience of all.
7. Fran's new record was ____________________________.
8. The dance tickets were ______________________________.
9. The tickets for the rock concert were the __________ of all.

DOUBLE NEGATIVES

Words such as **no** and forms of **no** are called negatives. Some common negatives are: no, not, none, nothing, never, nobody, and nowhere. *Only* **one** *negative can be used in a sentence.*

Example:

I do not want (*any, no*) pizza.

Notice: ***Not*** *and* ***No*** *are both negatives. Only one negative can be used.*

Copy the following sentences onto a separate sheet of paper and choose the correct word for each sentence. Make sure you have only one negative in each sentence.

1. I haven't read (no, any) books about stamp collecting.
2. When Kathy went on a diet, she didn't eat (anything, nothing) for one day.
3. Tony hadn't finished (none, any) of his homework.
4. Sally had not seen (no, any) of her friends during vacation.
5. Can't you find (nobody, anybody) to camp with us?
6. My friends wouldn't (ever, never) hurt me.
7. Our family didn't go (anywhere, nowhere) during the summer.
8. Nobody (can, can't) figure out that math problem.
9. Alice wouldn't go (nowhere, anywhere) without her best friend.
10. Marty couldn't buy (any, no) new clothes until she repaid her mother.

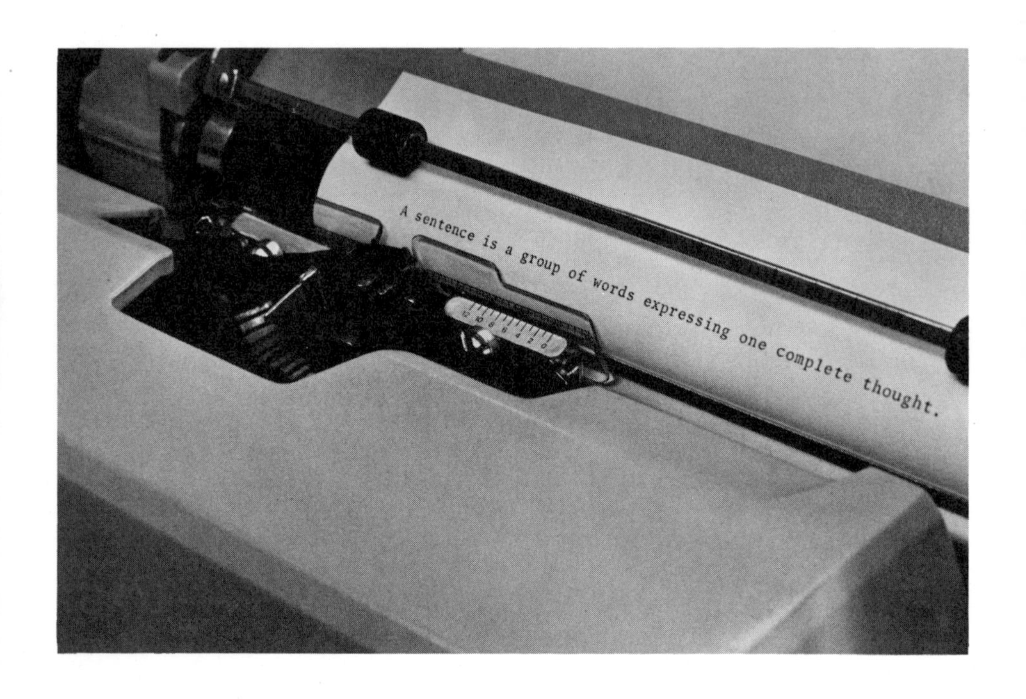

Chapter SEVEN

HOW MUCH DO I KNOW ABOUT SENTENCES?

"Someone's been smoking in the washroom," Mr. Josephson, the counselor, explained to Mark. "Were you in there last hour?"

"Yes and no," Mark mumbled.

On the basis of that incomplete reply, Mark could be in trouble. He should have said, "Yes, I went in there briefly, but I left when I saw one of the guys pass out cigarettes. No, I wasn't smoking." He could have cleared himself.

FRAGMENTS/COMPLETE SENTENCES

To make ourselves understood, we need to express ourselves in complete thoughts. A sentence is a group of words expressing one complete thought. If a thought is not complete, it is only a part of a sentence, called a sentence fragment.

Decide which groups of words below are fragments. On a separate sheet of paper, write down their numbers. Then, make sentences out of them by adding more words to express a complete thought.

1. Doctors have found that smoking is bad for your health.
2. Causes lung cancer.
3. Lighting matches and smoking can cause fires.
4. Emphysema is a lung disease often caused by smoking.
5. Is an expensive habit.
6. Smoking a cigarette.
7. Smoking can turn a person's lungs black.
8. Smells bad, too.
9. Save your health and money by not smoking.
10. Smoking causes heart disease.

FOUR KINDS OF SENTENCES

Sentences have four purposes:

(1) *to make statements*	(telling)
(2) *to ask questions*	(asking)
(3) *to show excitement*	(showing strong feeling)
(4) *to give commands*	(ordering someone to do something)

There are **four** kinds of sentences.

A telling sentence is called *declarative* and ends with a period. **(.)**

An asking sentence is called *interrogative* and ends with a question mark. **(?)**

A strong feeling sentence showing excitement is called *exclamatory* and ends with an exclamation mark. **(!)**

A command sentence, telling someone to do something, is called *imperative* and ends with a period or an exclamation mark. **(!)**

Copy the following sentences onto a separate sheet of paper. Put in the proper mark of punctuation at the end of each sentence. Then tell what kind of sentence each one is.

1. The Statue of Liberty is on a small island in New York Harbor
2. What a great sight to see this huge bronze statue of a woman holding a torch in one hand and a book in the other
3. Did you know the French people gave the statue as a present to the American people
4. Auguste Bartholdi designed this gigantic statue
5. The statue and pedestal stand 305 feet, 6 inches high
6. Can you imagine, the arm alone is 42 feet long
7. To get a close look at the Statue, a visitor must take a fifteen minute boat ride to the island
8. What a climb to go up the narrow winding staircase of 350 steps into the head of the Statue

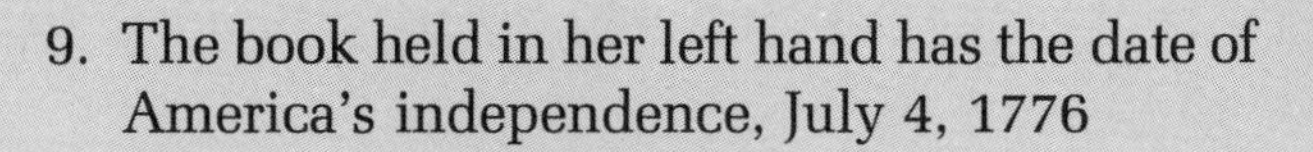

9. The book held in her left hand has the date of America's independence, July 4, 1776
10. What do travelers see first when they come by boat into New York
11. The Statue is a symbol of freedom and liberty in the United States
12. Go and see the Statue someday if you get a chance

RUN-ON SENTENCES

Every sentence must have a punctuation mark to show that the sentence is complete. Each new sentence begins with a capital letter.

Practice Punctuating and Capitalizing Sentences

In the following paragraph, all the sentences run together. There are no end punctuation marks which tell us where the sentences end. Copy the paragraph onto a separate sheet of paper. Put in all end punctuation marks and capital letters. You will have eleven sentences when you finish.

Every American should sometime visit Yellowstone National Park it covers an area that reaches into the three states of Montana, Wyoming, and Idaho Yellowstone National Park includes 2,213,206.55 acres many mountain ranges and pine forests surround the park the animal life, such as elk, deer, antelope, foxes, panthers, mountain sheep, and wolves are carefully protected by government forest rangers colorful flowers are everywhere during the summer months there are over 200 species of birds found in the park in addition, fish are plentiful in the many mountain streams that flow through the Park it's an amazing sight to see hot steam and boiling water shoot up into the air from the 3000 geysers and hot springs Old Faithful is the most famous geyser in the Park it is called Old Faithful because approximately every hour it shoots streams of hot water 130 feet into the air.

Did you find the eleven sentences? Does each sentence begin with a capital letter? Is the end punctuation at the end of each complete thought?

More Practice Punctuating and Capitalizing Sentences

Find twelve sentences in the following paragraph. Copy the paragraph onto a separate sheet of paper and start each new sentence with a capital letter. Don't forget the end punctuation marks.

I want to find a job for after school and weekends where do you work I've read so many want ads, but I haven't found anything Kathy got a job at the movie theater tonight I'm going to apply there the department store, the grocery store, or the restaurant might need someone I'll try every store in the shopping center how did you find your job job applications shouldn't be hard to fill out interviews make me nervous, but I must show them how hard I will work I know I'll find something just think of all the money I will make

SUBJECT-VERB AGREEMENT

Which is correct here?

1. Donna **is** working in the library.
2. Donna **are** working in the library.

Yes, number 1 is correct. Donna is a singular subject, and the singular verb **is** agrees with it.

Which sentence is correct?

1. The two boys **is** working in the cafeteria at lunchtime.
2. The two boys **are** working in the cafeteria at lunchtime.

That's right, number 2 is correct. Do you know why? The word **boys** is plural. The word boys means more than one boy. Therefore, the verb must be plural, also. The verb **are** is the plural form of the verb **is**.

Remember—1. *A singular subject needs a singular verb.*
2. *A plural subject needs a plural verb.*

Here are some common singular and plural verbs:

Singular	Plural
is	are
was	were
has	have
does	do

Copy the following sentences onto a separate sheet of paper. Choose the correct verb to match the subject in each sentence.

1. Football (is, are) played in the fall of the year.
2. In our school, many students (is, are) active in the Pep Club.
3. Last year our school (was, were) runner-up for the championship.
4. We (was, were) so disappointed when we lost our final game.
5. Swimming (has, have) become very popular recently.
6. In gym, the volleyball teams (has, have) played many games.
7. (Do, Does) your sister play tennis?
8. The gym classes (do, does) give instruction in golf.

COMPOUND SUBJECT-VERB AGREEMENT

Which sentence is correct? Should you use a singular or a plural verb?

1. Helen and Jim **is** working in the school office.
2. Helen and Jim **are** working in the school office.

Number 2 is correct because there are two (compound) subjects joined with the word **and.** There are two people working in the office, so a plural verb is needed.

Which is correct here?

1. Bob or Janet **is** going to get the job at the department store.
2. Bob or Janet **are** going to get the job at the department store.

Number 1 is correct. The word **or** joins the two subjects. This means that only one person will get the job, so a singular verb is needed.

Remember—1. *A compound subject joined with the word* **and** *needs a plural verb.*

2. *A compound subject joined with the word* **or** *needs a singular verb.*

In the following sentences, which verbs are correct? Copy the sentences onto a separate sheet of paper and use the correct verb in each sentence.

1. Clean air and water (is, are) important to our health.
2. Automobiles and trucks (is, are) responsible for part of the pollution problem.
3. Which (is, are) more responsible for air pollution—a factory or a school?
4. New cars (has, have) devices to help stop pollution.
5. Polluted air (has, have) made many people sick.
6. Dead fish and "No Swimming" signs (was, were) seen all along the beach.
7. Air pollution or water pollution (is, are) going to be the project for the Ecology Club.
8. Noise pollution and litter (do, does) concern many people in our community.
9. Using up our national resources or just wasting them (do, does) affect everyone.

YOU (SUBJECT-VERB AGREEMENT)

Which is correct?

1. You **is** coming to the dance.
2. You **are** coming to the dance.

That's right. Number 2 is correct. When the word <u>you</u> is the subject of the sentence, a plural verb is needed. The word <u>you</u>, as a subject of a sentence, always takes a plural verb, whether <u>you</u> talks about one person or several people.

Remember—*When the subject of a sentence is* *you,* *a plural verb is needed.*

Copy the following sentences onto a separate sheet of paper, and choose the correct verb for each sentence.

1. Imagine you (is, are) going on a vacation.
2. (Has, Have) you locked all the windows?
3. (Was, Were) you careful to stop your newspaper delivery?
4. (Does, Do) you ask your neighbor to watch the house for you?

SUBJECT-VERB AGREEMENT REVIEW

When you are not sure which verb is correct, say aloud the subject together with each verb and listen. Your ear will tell you which is correct. Which sounds right to you?

1. Jerry **play** tennis every day after school.
2. Jerry **plays** tennis everyday at school.

Yes, number 2 is correct because it sounds right.

Remember—*When in doubt, say the subject and verb together and see which sounds correct.*

Copy the following sentences onto a separate sheet of paper. Choose the correct verb for each sentence.

1. Melissa and Karen (shop, shops) for food for their party.
2. They (buy, buys) food to make tacos.
3. Melissa (grate, grates) the cheese, (chop, chops) the green peppers, (slice, slices) the tomatoes, and (cook, cooks) the meat.
4. Karen (prepare, prepares) the lettuce, onions, taco sauce, and the taco shells.
5. All the kids (make, makes) their own tacos at the party.
6. These tacos (taste, tastes) great!

CONTRACTION AGREEMENT

The singular or plural form of a verb does not change when the contraction n't is added to the verb. Here are some common singular and plural contractions:

Singular	**Plural**
isn't	aren't
wasn't	weren't
hasn't	haven't
doesn't	don't

Copy the following sentences onto a separate sheet of paper and choose the correct contraction for each sentence. Remember that the verb must agree with the subject.

1. Ocean liners today (isn't, aren't) used only for shipping goods from one country to another.
2. (Hasn't, Haven't) you seen a huge ocean liner that carries over a thousand people across the ocean?
3. It (don't, doesn't) seem possible that there could be such a huge floating hotel.
4. If you think they only provide places to sleep, they (don't, doesn't).
5. There (isn't, aren't) anything missing: excellent food, dancing, swimming—indoors and out—movies, church services, a library, gift shop, beauty shop, small gym, skeet shooting, shuffleboard, table tennis, talent shows, a large game room, a doctor, and a small operating room.
6. I've had so much fun in the nightclubs, that I (hasn't, haven't) had much time to sleep.
7. There (wasn't, weren't) enough time in a six-day crossing to do everything.
8. After spending so many days on water, there (wasn't, weren't) a more exciting moment than to first see land.

SENTENCE STRUCTURE

CONJUNCTIONS

Listen to a young child talk. Notice that the sentences are very short because the ideas are very simple. The following are simple sentences because they each express one thought. A young child might say, "Mom, camp is fun. We go horseback riding every morning. I swim and fish every day. We go on nature walks. The food is good."

As a person grows, the ideas and language grow, and the sentences become longer and more interesting. A compound sentence expresses two complete thoughts joined together with one of the connecting words. These words are called conjunctions. The most common conjunctions are **and, but, or, nor.**

The simple sentences above can now become one sentence when spoken by a young adult. "Mom, camp is fun, **and** I enjoy horseback riding, swimming, fishing, nature walks, and the food." Note that the conjunction **and** joins the simple sentences. "Mom, camp is fun," is one complete sentence. "I enjoy horseback riding, swimming, fishing, nature walks, and the food," is another simple sentence. The conjunction **and** joins both simple sentences together. Notice that a comma goes before the conjunction. Both sentences are talking about the same subject—camp. The ideas in both sentences are related.

How well can you join the following related ideas together, using **and, but, or, nor?**

Copy the following sentences onto a separate sheet of paper, and use one of the conjunctions to connect the two simple sentences into one.

1. I packed all my things for camp, ______ I did not forget my toothbrush.
2. Camp will be lots of fun, ______ I will miss my family.
3. Mother said I could go to camp, ______ I could visit my grandfather's farm.

4. You wouldn't turn down a trip to camp, ______ would I.
5. I took the bus to camp, ______ it took three hours.
6. Canoeing is fun, ______ I like archery better.
7. Camp food is good, ______ Mom's is better.
8. In the afternoon, mail comes, ______ I was so happy to get the box of cookies from home.
9. On Wednesday, we could sing around the campfire, ______ we could go to town for a movie.
10. I learned how to cast, ______ I can hardly wait to show Dad the next time we go fishing.

Remember—*1. Be sure to put a comma* before *the conjunction in a compound sentence.*

2. The two sentences that are joined together must be related to the same subject.

VARYING SENTENCE PATTERNS

SENTENCES BEGINNING WITH PHRASES

Now that you've learned to make longer and more interesting sentences, there is still another way to show you've grown in your thinking ability.

It is easy to get into the habit of having all our sentences fall into the same pattern of a subject followed by a verb. This is dull to read. There are ways of rearranging words and using different word patterns. One way is to start a sentence with a **phrase** using a word chosen from the following groups of words.

I	above	across	against	along	around	at
II	before	behind	below	beneath	beyond	
	beside	between	by			
III	down	during				
IV	except					

V	for	from		
VI	in	into		
VII	of	off	on	over
VII	through	throughout	to	toward
IX	under	underneath	until	up
X	with	within	without	

Notice that these sentences begin with phrases using words from Section I. They do not begin with the subject of the sentence.

1. (**Above** the trees,) the sound of birds could be heard.
2. (**Across** the street,) ran the brown puppy.
3. (**Against** the fence,) leaned the tired old man.
4. (**Along** the road,) a snake crawled.
5. (**Around** the house,) many jobs had to be done.
6. (**At** the store,) we bought bread.

Below are some phrases made up of prepositions from Section II. On a separate sheet of paper, complete each sentence by adding words to make a complete thought.

1. Before school, ________________.
2. Behind the garage, ________________.
3. Below the ground, ________________.
4. Beneath the shelves, ________________.
5. Beside the desk, ________________.
6. Between the cars, ________________.
7. Beyond the mountain, ________________.
8. By the road, ________________.

Use the prepositions in the remaining Sections III through X, and make up your own phrases. Orally use the phrases at the beginning of sentences.

SENTENCES BEGINNING WITH SUBORDINATE CONJUNCTIONS

Another way to make sentences interesting is to begin them with subordinate conjunctions. The most common ones are:

since	while	as	when	after
before	whether	although	if	because

These words can be used to start sentences.

Examples:

1. **Since** it was raining, he took a cab to the station.
2. **When** the party was over, everyone went home.
3. **Whether** you graduate from high school or not, it is important to learn a trade or a work skill.
4. **While** you drive a car, watch out for other drivers.

Remember—*Put a comma where you would normally pause when speaking.*

On a separate sheet of paper, write six sentences. Begin each sentence with one of the remaining subordinate conjunctions listed above.

SENTENCES BEGINNING WITH "ING" WORDS

The third way to add variety to sentences is to start them with action words that end in **ing.** When action words ending in "ing" are used as nouns, they are called gerunds.

Examples:

1. **Swimming** across the lake to the island was a great achievement.
2. **Looking** for fossils at the quarry was a new experience for our class.
3. **Eating** at the restaurant was a treat for the family.

On a separate sheet of paper, write five sentences. Start each sentence with one of the following **ing** words.

running studying working driving watching

Chapter EIGHT

PARAGRAPH–WHAT IS IT?

THE TOPIC OF A PARAGRAPH

Often one sentence cannot tell what we are trying to express. Therefore, we must use several sentences. That's what a paragraph is—several sentences about one idea.

What is the topic of the following paragraph?

More than 50,000 bicycles were purchased in the city of Chicago during a one year period. These travel and recreation vehicles have become very popular recently. With so much traffic, high parking costs, and gasoline shortages, many people now use bicycles to get back and forth to work.

Remember—1. *All the sentences in a paragraph must be about the same subject. In the above paragraph, every sentence is about bicycles.*

2. *The first sentence of each paragraph starts in a little from the left margin. This is called indenting.*

Here is an example of a paragraph which is made up of several sentences about one main idea. Three of the sentences have nothing to do with the main idea. Can you find them?

Buying a house involves many things. You may find a house for sale through a real estate agent. Or, the owner of a house who wants to sell it may advertise it for sale in the local newspaper. Birds often build nests in trees near houses. Some people will not buy a house unless there is a garage for a car. Some houses have air conditioning and a wood-burning fireplace. People who have children make sure that the house is near school. Also, it is important that the house has enough closets for clothes. People who keep up with fashions have many clothes. If the family is large, the house should have enough bedrooms. It is also important that a house has a yard for children to play. The children enjoy playing.

Which sentences in the following paragraphs do not belong because they are not part of the topic of the paragraph?

There are lots of decisions to make when you purchase a bicycle. You must decide if you want a touring or racing model. Racing bikes have dropped handle bars. Many people say they are more comfortable for long trips. Juan has a blue one. Next, you must decide how many speeds you want. Having different gears makes pedalling a lot easier. A garage is a good place to keep a car. Also, there are many different brands of bicycles. Checking out bike shops, department stores, and discount stores can help you decide which bike to buy. My reflector fell off my bike last week.

METHODS OF ORGANIZATION

TIME ORDER WORDS

Sentences in a paragraph must express ideas in an understandable order so that the person who reads the material can follow what the writer is trying to say. Certain words are helpful to make your ideas follow this natural order of development. The easiest way of telling how something happened is to give the events in the order in which they occured.

The following words are used to show this time order of events.

first meanwhile later then afterward finally

The sample paragraph below shows the use of these words.

First, the alarm went off at 6:00 A.M. I dressed and rushed to get my room in order. **Meanwhile,** Mom was downstairs making breakfast. Hurriedly, I ate breakfast. **Then,** I rushed out to the garage and put my books in my bike bag. **Later,** on my way to school, I heard a hissing noise. It was a flat! Our neighbor came to my rescue with a patch and a hand pump. **Afterward,** I continued on. **Finally,** I arrived at school, thirty-five minutes late!

Remember—*The sentences in a paragraph must follow the natural time order.*

Rewrite the following paragraph on a separate sheet of paper, and put the sentences in the correct time order.

Then, just before we were dismissed, the principal reminded us not to forget our graduation gowns and to be in the gym by 6:30 that night. Meanwhile, the President of the School Board was in the office signing all our diplomas. Finally, we were dismissed and some of us went out for pizza and cokes. Later, after we had marched down the aisle twice, we were assigned seats in the front rows of the auditorium. First, I arrived at school for graduation practice.

LOCATION WORDS

Another group of words is very helpful when we try to describe the location of objects, and when we tell how their position is related to other things nearby. These key words are used:

next to **in front of** **beside** **nearby** **between** **behind**

The sample paragraph below shows the use of these words.

The new library has just been opened to the public. It is a beautiful building near the center of town. **Between** the front door and the side entrance to the library is a staircase which leads to the art gallery below. **Beside** the parking lot is a book drop to be used after closing hours. **Next to** the parking lot is the local swimming center. **Behind** the library are four tennis courts. **Nearby** are the fire and police departments.

LINKING IDEA WORDS

Finally, there are words we use to connect ideas from one sentence to the other. These key words are used:

however	**furthermore**	**as a result**
nevertheless	**in fact**	**therefore**

Copy the following paragraph onto a separate sheet of paper. Use the words listed above in the blank spaces. Read each sentence with your choice. Does it make sense?

There is a lot of violence on TV and in the movies. ________ of this, many people think crime has increased. ________, do you realize that in the big cities crime has almost doubled? ________, people still shop at night and do not seem to be afraid. ________, some people are worried that their children are influenced by all this violence. ________, they think that something should be done.

PARAGRAPH WRITING

Now you are ready to write your own paragraph. Remember to use time order words, location words, and linking idea words to express your thoughts clearly.

Pick a topic from the selection below, and, on a separate sheet of paper, write a one-paragraph description of it.

A MOVIE

A CAR

LAST CHRISTMAS

A FAVORITE FOOD

A NEW OUTFIT

Chapter NINE

CAN I WRITE SEVERAL PARAGRAPHS ON ONE TOPIC?

A COMPOSITION

In the last chapter, we learned that a paragraph has one main idea. Now, let's write three paragraphs on one subject. This is called a composition. To write a composition, we must organize all our ideas and plan which details to include in each paragraph.

Think about the topic—**A Car of My Own**. Let's write a composition. In the first paragraph, explain why the car is needed. Is it needed for work, recreation, school, errands, or shopping?

In the second paragraph, explain how one could buy the car. Could money be saved by working or from one's allowance? Should a person buy a car from a car dealer, a used car lot, or a person who advertises in the newspaper?

Finally, in the third paragraph, describe the responsibilities that a person has in owning and driving a car. How does a person pass a driving test and obtain a license, license plates, and a title to the car? How can one keep a car in good repair? Where and how does a person get insurance? What are important traffic laws? How can a person be a good and safe driver?

Remember—1. *Indent the first word in each paragraph.*

2. *Leave a one inch margin along each side of the page.*

On a separate sheet of paper, write the three paragraphs as outlined above on **A Car of My Own**. Write complete sentences using the details as suggested for each paragraph. You will then have a composition.

ORGANIZING PARAGRAPH DETAILS

Now that you know how the ideas in a composition are organized, you can write on any subject. Remember, organize the details for each paragraph before you start to write.

The following topics suggest many details. Which topic will you choose for your composition?

1. **My Best Date (or My Worst Date)**
   Paragraph Details
      Why was it?
      Describe what happened.
      How did you feel after the date?

2. **My Favorite Television Program**
   Paragraph Details
      Describe the program.
      Tell about the actors and actresses.
      Why is it your favorite?

3. **My Favorite Music**
   Paragraph Details
      Descibe the music.
      Tell about the recording artists.
      Tell about a concert or a favorite album.

4. **My Worst Fears**
   Paragraph Details
      Describe the fears.
      Why am I afraid?
      When and where have I felt this fear?

On a separate sheet of paper, write a composition. Choose one of the topics listed above for your topic.

OPEN-ENDED STORIES

The paragraphs below describe a situation that has no ending. Put yourself in the story. What would you do?

Ed is the star of the football team. Paul is his best friend. He's on the football team, too, but he never gets to play. Their English teacher told them to come to her room after school tonight, because she thinks they cheated on yesterday's exam. Paul knows he didn't cheat and is afraid that Ed copied from his paper. But, the championship game is next Friday. Paul knows that if Ed is found guilty of cheating, he'll be suspended from the team for the big game. Maybe he should take the blame and clear Ed.

If you were Paul, what would you do? On a separate sheet of paper, write your own ending for the story.

WRITING FROM PICTURES

Look at this picture. What is happening? What could have made her look this way?

On a separate sheet of paper, write a three paragraph story about this picture. These suggested details will help you to organize your thinking and writing for each paragraph.

Paragraph 1

-(The Situation) Why is she screaming? What kind of danger is there? How does she feel inside? Where is this happening?

Paragraph 2

-(Possible Solution) Can she run? Is she trapped? Is she alone? Is any help available? How can she help herself?

Paragraph 3

-(Solution) How does she solve her problem? Explain.

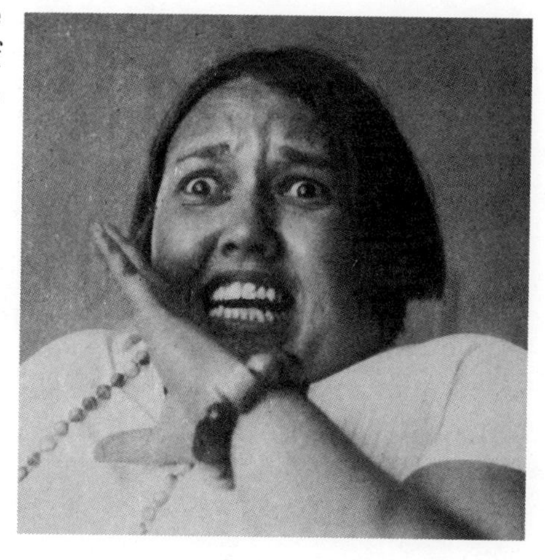

AN AUTOBIOGRAPHY

What is a biography? **Bio** is a Greek word that means life, and **graphim** is also a Greek word that means to write. Therefore, a biography is a story written about a person's life.

Do you know what the prefix **auto** means? It means self. Thus, an autobiography is the story written about one's own life.

You are going to write an autobiography about your own life. Include five chapters in your autobiography. Use this outline to organize your ideas for each chapter.

Remember—1. *Indent each paragraph.*

2. *Keep one inch margins.*
3. *Write complete sentences.*
4. *Begin each sentence with a capital.*
5. *End each sentence with a punctuation mark.*
6. *Be sure all sentences in each paragraph are on one topic.*
7. *Use good handwriting.*
8. *Read over each chapter and correct your mistakes before you hand it to your teacher.*

Outline For An Autobiography

I. My family
   A. Who is in my family?
   B. Tell about them

II. My childhood
   A. Interesting events I remember
   B. Think about those events
      1. Why do I remember them?
      2. Did they teach me a lesson?

III. My history
   A. Personal life
      1. Was I ever punished for something I didn't do?
      2. Things I did at home
   B. School
      1. School subjects
      2. Sports
      3. Others (attendance, awards for contests, etc.)

IV. Personal feelings
   A. Likes (TV shows, foods, clothing, etc.)
   B. Dislikes (TV shows, foods, clothing, etc.)

V. My future
   A. What do I hope to do when I graduate?
      1. Do my hopes fit my abilities? Why or why not?
      2. How can I reach my goals?
   B. What kind of person do I want to be? (honest, gentle, rough, dependable, etc.)

Chapter TEN

DO I KNOW HOW TO WRITE LETTERS?

Letters are an important form of communication. Of all forms of writing, a letter makes the most direct contact with the reader, especially those who live far away. Since a letter is designed for the reader, it should be very clear and easily understood.

FRIENDLY LETTERS

It is fun to talk with our friends. Sometimes, this is difficult to do because our friends don't live nearby. Maybe you have a friend in a place where you used to live, or maybe your best friend's family moved away. Letter writing can help you stay friends!

Letters to friends and relatives are called **friendly letters.** We try to express ourselves as though we were talking. It's such a good feeling to find a letter from a friend in the mailbox!

Look at the sample of the friendly letter on the next page. Note that there are five parts to a friendly letter. Look at the location of each part in the friendly letter on the opposite page.

① **Heading**—This is your address and the date when you wrote the letter. Your friend can write you a return letter, if you include your address.

② **Greeting**—This is like saying "hello" when you answer the phone.

③ **Body of Letter**—This is where you tell your friend about your activities and ideas.

④ **Closing**—This is like saying "good-bye."

⑤ **Your Name**—This is your signature and makes the letter personally from you.

⑥ **P. S.**—This is a post script. It is written after the close of a letter to add a message that you forgot in your letter.

On a separate sheet of paper, write a friendly letter to a friend or relative. Remember to include all five parts.

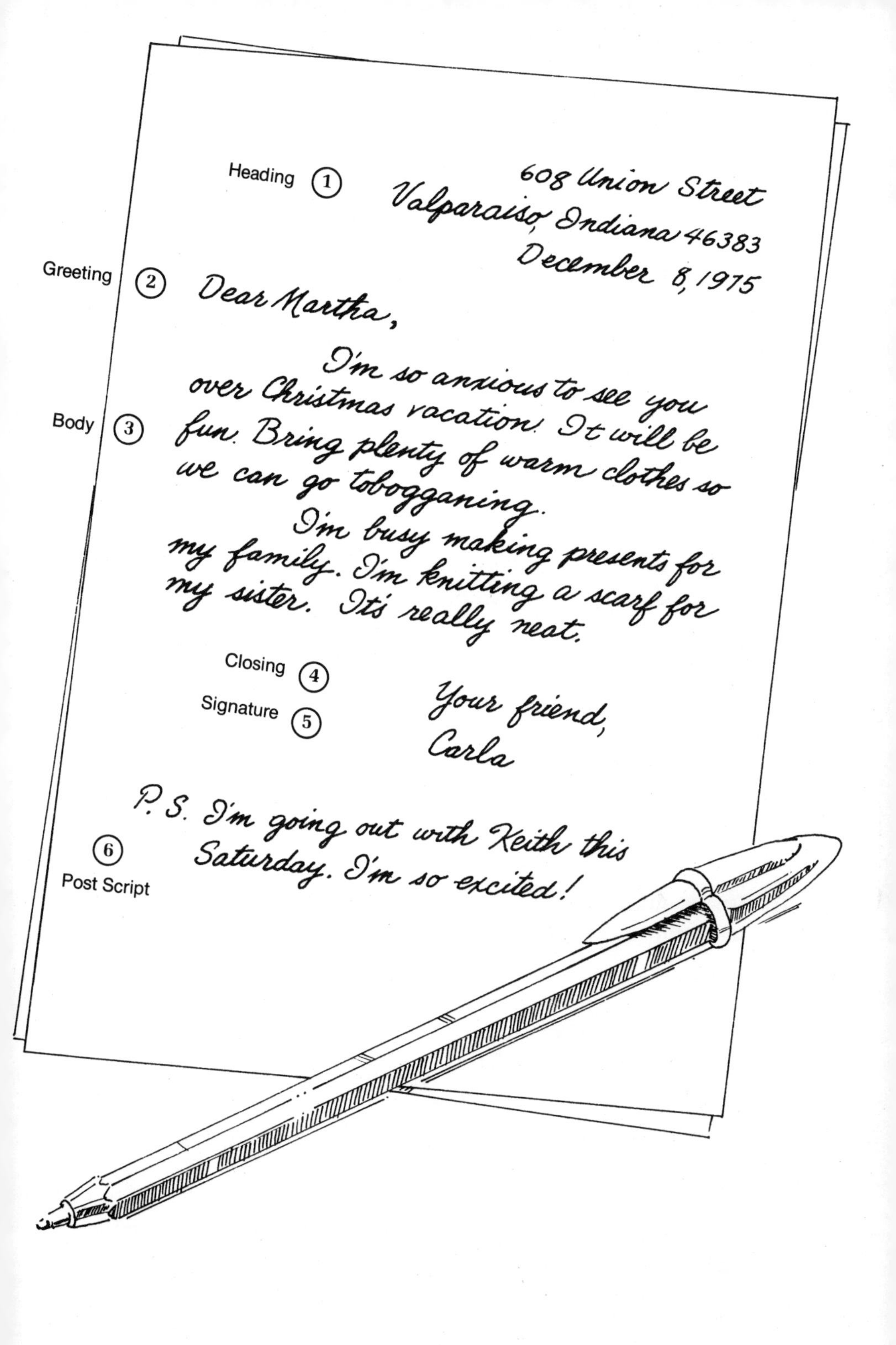
608 Union Street
Valparaiso, Indiana 46383
December 8, 1975

Dear Martha,

I'm so anxious to see you over Christmas vacation. It will be fun. Bring plenty of warm clothes so we can go tobogganing.

I'm busy making presents for my family. I'm knitting a scarf for my sister. It's really neat.

Your friend,
Carla

P.S. I'm going out with Keith this Saturday. I'm so excited!

BUSINESS LETTERS

We often need to communicate with people we do not know. Letters are often used when looking for a job or when buying things. These are called **business** letters.

Business letters usually ask for something which is important. The people who receive the letters are frequently very busy. Keep the letter as short as possible, state your ideas very clearly, and write neatly or use a typewriter. This will make your letter easy to read and understand.

Look at the sample of the business letter on the next page. Always use appropriate stationery, pay attention to margins and neatness, and number pages in the same order as a book. Note that there are six parts to a business letter. Look at the location of each part in the business letter on the opposite page.

① **Heading**—This is your address. Since business letters are often written to people you do not know, and since business letters usually demand a reply, your address is very important. Include the date you wrote the letter to make sure you get a prompt reply.

② **Inside Address**—This is the address of the person or business to whom you are writing.

③ **Greeting**—This is a formal way of saying hello. If you know the name of the person to whom you are writing, use it here; for example, **"Dear Mr. Miller:"**. If you don't know who will read your letter, use **"Dear Sir or Madam:"**.

④ **Body of letter**—This is where you state your ideas and facts, clearly and neatly.

⑤ **Closing**—This is a formal good-bye or ending of the letter.

⑥ **Your Name**—This shows who the letter is from. Your signature makes the letter official. Print or type your name under your signature, so it is easy to read. Use your full name. Don't use a nickname.

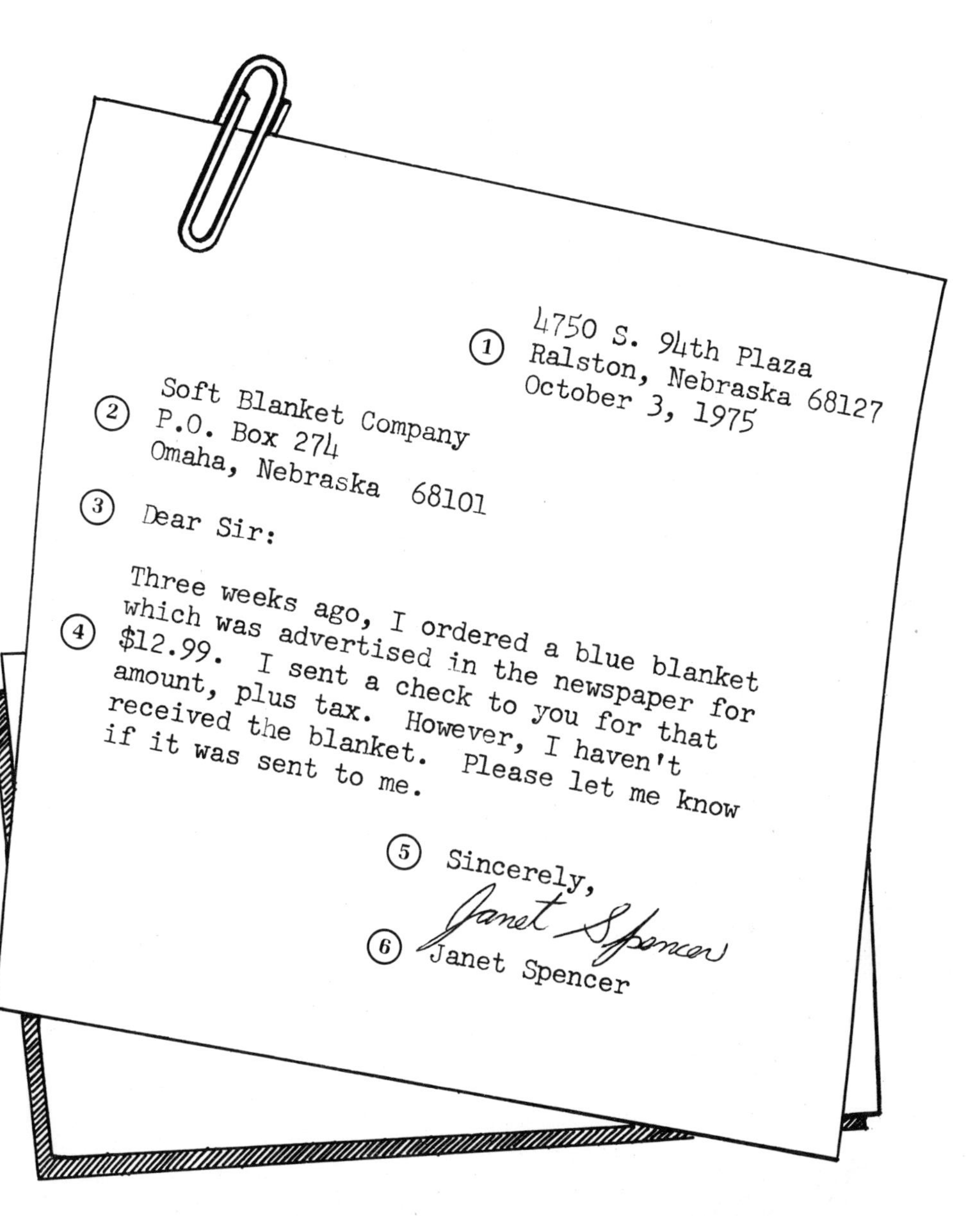
4750 S. 94th Plaza
Ralston, Nebraska 68127
October 3, 1975

Soft Blanket Company
P.O. Box 274
Omaha, Nebraska 68101

Dear Sir:

Three weeks ago, I ordered a blue blanket which was advertised in the newspaper for $12.99. I sent a check to you for that amount, plus tax. However, I haven't received the blanket. Please let me know if it was sent to me.

Sincerely,

Janet Spencer

Janet Spencer

Write a business letter to the Good-Value Department Store at 6305 South Hillside Avenue, Chicago, Illinois. The zip code is 60235. In your letter, explain that you bought a portable radio from them three months ago and that it doesn't work anymore. It has a one year guarantee. Ask them what they will do. Include all facts and details which you think are important.

ENVELOPES

Envelopes must be clearly and accurately written so that the post office can determine where a letter is to be sent.

Envelopes for friendly letters and business letters use the same form.

(1) **Return Address**—This is your name and address. If your letter cannot be delivered, it will be returned to you. Without a return address, it will end up in a dead letter office. Don't forget your zip code.

(2) **Mailing Address**—This is where the letter is going. Write clearly and accurately. Every number is important. Don't forget the zip code.

(3) **Postage**—This is the stamp for the class and weight of your letter. Most letters weigh less than ½ ounce and are sent first class for the quickest delivery. Don't forget that it costs extra to send letters special delivery.

(4) **Special Instructions**—This is where you tell the post office any special instructions; such as, "Special Delivery" or "Do not bend."

Write an envelope for the business letter you wrote to the Good-Value Department Store. Include all four parts.

SOCIAL NOTES

Social notes are really friendly letters, with one important difference. The friendly letter can talk about many things. Generally, it's an exchange of much news and ideas. The social note, however, contains a specific message written to meet the needs of a specific social situation. For example, invitations to dinners, meetings, or replies to invitations are social notes. Thank-you notes can be included, too.

Except for the message, the social note follows the same pattern or form as the friendly letter.

Chapter ELEVEN

DO I KNOW HOW TO FILL OUT FORMS?

As a part of our everyday living, we must fill out many forms. Forms ask us questions for a specific purpose. Some purposes are applying for a job, a charge account, or public assistance. We usually fill out forms to get something we need or want. Therefore, it is important to follow the directions, answer all questions correctly, and write neatly.

EMPLOYMENT APPLICATIONS

When applying for a job, it is usually necessary to fill out a form called an employment application. It is important to do your best when filling out this form, so that you will be considered for the job. It is most important to answer every question honestly.

Job applications are not difficult to fill out. Most businesses use the same type of form. There are several words which appear frequently on these forms which you should know. The application form on the next page is divided into six sections. Some terms used in each section are defined below.

Personal information:—who are you?
dependents—people who need you to support them.
citizen of United States—people born in the U.S. or who have pledged their loyalty to this country.

Employment desired:—what job do you want to apply for?

Education:—what training have you had, and how far have you gone in school?

Previous experience:—who have you worked for in the past?

References:—what people know you well and can tell about you?

Physical record:—in what condition is your body?
physical defects—things wrong with your body.
in case of emergency notify—someone to call if you get sick or have an accident while you are working.

SAMPLE FORM

APPLICATION FOR EMPLOYMENT

PERSONAL INFORMATION — Date ....

NAME IN FULL .... SOCIAL SECURITY NO. ....

Address .... Phone Own .... Neighbor ....

City .... State .... ZIP CODE ....

How long have you lived in this City? .... This State? .... Citizen of United States? ....

Age ...... Birthday: Month .... Day .... Year .... Sex .... Weight .... Height ....

☐ Married ☐ Single No. of Children .... Ages: .... Other Dependents ....

If Married, state employment of Spouse ....

Employment desired .... **Wages Expected** .... Per Hour

What other work can you do? ....

EDUCATION

School	DATE From	DATE To	Name of School	City and State	Course	Did You Graduate?
Grammar						
High						
College						
Other						

PREVIOUS EXPERIENCE *(Give names and addresses of previous employers)*

	Name and Address of Employer	DATE From	DATE To	List Duties Performed	Starting Wages	Final Wages	Reason for Leaving
1	....						
2	....						

REFERENCES: *Give below the names of three persons not related to you, whom you have known at least one year.*

	NAME	ADDRESS	BUSINESS	YEARS ACQUAINTED
1				
2				
3				

PHYSICAL RECORD

Have you any physical defects? .... If so, what? .... Wear glasses? ....

Are you now employed? .... Where? ....

In case of emergency notify ....

Name ADDRESS PHONE NO.

I understand that misrepresentation or omission of facts called for is cause for dismissal. Further, I understand and agree that my employment is for no definite period and may, regardless of the date of payment of my wages and salary, be terminated at any time without any previous notice.

Witness .... **Sign Here** ....

DO NOT WRITE BELOW THIS LINE

Interviewed by .... Date .... Hour ....

Remarks: ....

Occupation .... Dept. .... Starting Date .... Starting Rate ....

All qualified applicants will receive consideration without regard to age, race, color, religion, sex, national origin or military status.

SAMPLE FORM

There is a statement at the bottom of this application form. You must always read a statement before you sign your name. Your signature makes your application official and tells the business that you have filled out the form correctly and honestly.

misrepresentation —not telling the truth
omission ————leaving out important information
dismissal————being fired from a job
terminated ————ended
previous notice ——told ahead of time

On a separate sheet of paper, make an application for employment. Include only the sections on **Personal Information, Education,** and **References.** Fill in the application form as though you were really applying for a job.

CATALOG ORDERS

Many stores offer people a way to make purchases by mail. Many people find this a convenient, easy and fun way to shop. Sears and Roebuck, J. C. Penney and Montgomery Ward are three stores that offer large catalogs to their customers. These catalogs give all the information a person needs to shop at home. There are pictures and descriptions of all the products.

Solid-state receiver has vernier slide-rule tuning, switched AFC to reduce FM drifting and FM stereo indicator light. Slide controls for bass, treble, balance and volume. Built-in jacks for tape deck, headphones and speakers. **8-track recorder/player** comes with 2 mikes for live stereo recordings; or record directly from receiver or auxiliary units. Fast forward control brings you to any spot on your tapes in seconds. Auto-Stop 1 & 4 records 1 program at a time or all 4 continuously. Built-in ALC sets each channel's volume as you record. Record indicator light lets you know when you're recording. Manual or automatic track selection; lighted track indicators. Incl. blank tape. **Speakers** each contains 5-in. woofer and two 3-in. tweeters; 19½x11½x6⅝ in. Unit: 4½x19¾x9¼ in. UL listed. See (*) below left.
62 C 6244 AS—Wt. 37 lbs. **197.95**

100% cotton printed flannel

C **WARMTH WITHOUT WEIGHT.** 100% cotton printed flannel shirt. Full cut. Long tails. Fashion length collar, two button-thru pockets. Double-stitched mainseams. Maximum shrinkage 2-3%. Machine wash, warm; tumble dry. Made in Hong Kong. **Colors** • 50 blue • 10 red • 40 green.
Sizes: **S, M, L, XL.** Shipping weight each 14 oz. **State color number and size letter S, M, L, XL—not number size,** see chart.
B 42 C 889 D. . . . . **2** for **8.14**; Ea. **4.47**

Look at the sample catalog pages. They contain merchandise from several pages of a Montgomery Ward catalog. Notice all the information that is given. Each item is described showing the colors and sizes available, the catalog number, the price, and the weight of the item.

Shiny aluminum cookware 24.95 8-pc. set

E **Cast aluminum cookware rapidly transfers heat** to all sides of a vessel to evenly surround food being cooked—no "hot spots" that scorch and burn. Cook waterless—clear glass covers fit snugly inside the vessels to form a seal as the food heats so natural juices condense on the lids, continually basting foods in their own rich flavor. Pebbled finish exteriors; slick, smooth interiors. 8-pc. set: 1½- and 2-qt. cov'd saucepans, 5-qt. cov'd Dutch oven, 8- and 10-in. open skillets.

86 C 20648 M—Ship. wt. 13 lbs. 8 oz. .... set **24.95**

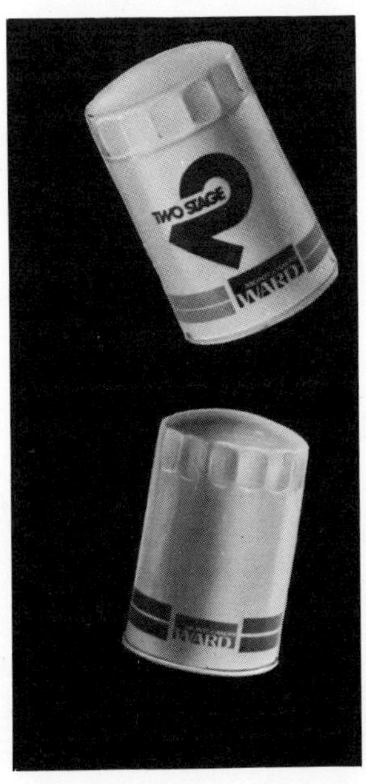

OIL FILTERS For these makes, years and models	2 Stage Cat. no.	Each
AMC (All) 1970–74 V-8; 1965–74 6 cyl.	61 C 39153	**3.79**
1975 V-8 and 6 cyl.	61 C 39155	**3.79**
Buick (All) 1961–66 All 6 cyl. and V-8	61 C 39153	**3.79**
1967 6-cyl.; 1967–75 V-8	61 C 39155	**3.79**
1968 6-cyl.	61 C 39154	**3.79**
1969–75 6 cyl.	61 C 39154	**3.79**
1975 All w/231 6 cyl. (exc. Skyhawk)	61 C 39155	**3.79**
Cadillac 1960–67	61 C 39153	**3.79**
1968–75	61 C 39155	**3.79**
Chevrolet (All) 1958–67 V-8 (except Chevy II)	....	.....
1962–68 6 cyl. (except Corvair)	61 C 39154	**3.79**
1964–67 Chevy II V-8	61 C 39154	**3.79**
1968 V-8	61 C 39154	**3.79**
1969–75 V-8	61 C 39154	**3.79**
1969–75 6-cylinder (except Corvair)	61 C 39154	**3.79**
1971–75 4-cylinder Vega	61 C 39154	**3.79**
Chevrolet Truck		
1960–75 V-8 Series 10 thru 30; El Camino, Blazer		
with Spin-on Type	61 C 39154	**3.79**
with Element Type	....	.....
1960–68 6 cyl. Series 10 thru 30; El Camino Blazer		
with Spin-on Type	61 C 39154	**3.79**
with Element Type	....	.....
1969–75 6 cylinder Series 10 thru 30; El Camino, Blazer	61 C 39154	**3.79**
Chrysler (All Chrysler products, Dodge, Plymouth, etc.)		
1960–72 (except Dodge Colt)	61 C 39151	**3.79**
1973–75 (except Dodge Colt)	61 C 39152	**3.79**
Datsun 1955–67 1500, 1600; 1966 on L-520	....	.....
1968–75 models w/Spin-on Filter 15208-65002; PL 510 w/1600 cc Engine	61 C 39151	**3.79**

SAMPLE PAGE

SEND TO: MONTGOMERY WARD, CHICAGO, ILL. 60607

ORDER BLANK & CHANGE-OF-ADDRESS NOTICE*

***If Wards does not have your CORRECT PRESENT address, please fill-in #1 and #2 below, and mail to Wards.** Date______

COMBINE ORDERS, AND SAVE!

You save time and money by combining purchases in a single order. Your transportation cost generally will be lower than on these same purchases, ordered separately. You may also save when you combine your orders for larger, unmailable merchandise. (Items with catalog numbers ending in "R" or "F".) Since the truck and express companies charge for a specific minimum poundage, even if shipment weighs less, you can order additional items (up to this minimum) with no increase in your shipping cost. See opposite page for details.

PLEASE PRINT ALL INFORMATION (INCLUDING A CHANGE OF ADDRESS)

#1. MY PRESENT NAME, ADDRESS

Name______ (first) (middle) (last)

Address______ Apt. No.______

City______ State______

ZIP code______ Phone______

#2. MY PREVIOUS ADDRESS

(Fill-in only if Wards does not have your CORRECT PRESENT address.)

Address______ Apt. No.______

City______

State______ ZIP code______

METHOD OF PAYMENT

☐ PLEASE OPEN AN ACCOUNT. I am submitting the completed application form on pages 939, 940.

☐ ADD TO MY CHARG-ALL ACCOUNT
My account number is______

Wards store or Catalog House where my account is carried______

☐ CASH (check or money order enclosed)

☐ SPECIAL INSTRUCTIONS______

This purchase is made at a time sale price, consisting of the cash sale price and a time price differential or **finance charge** and is subject to the terms and conditions of my Credit Agreement with you.

SIGNATURE (Sign full name as shown on your account)

PLEASE DO NOT WRITE IN THIS SPACE

SHIP TO ANOTHER ADDRESS

Name______

Address______ Apt. No.______

City______ State______

ZIP code______ Phone______

GIVE COMPLETE CATALOG NUMBER. Do you have a credit account? It's the convenient way to shop. Check box above.	HOW MANY	ITEM	COLOR NUMBER	SIZE or other code number	PRICE EACH	TOTAL PRICE	SHIP. WT. (Fill-in for cash orders only.) LBS.	OZ.

TAX (subject to change by State and/or Local governments)

Alabama*: 4%; Georgia*: 3%; Illinois: 5% (state and local); Indiana: 4%; Iowa: 3%; Kentucky: 5%; Michigan: 4%; Mississippi: 5%; Missouri: 3%; Ohio*: 4%; Tennessee*: 3½%; Wisconsin: 4%.
*Add local tax, if applicable in your locality.

FILL IN FOR CASH ORDERS ONLY

ON CREDIT ORDERS WARDS FIGURES THESE CHARGES.

			Total lbs.	Total oz.
TOTAL FOR GOODS				
TAX (see at left)				
POSTAGE (see opposite page)				
Owed on previous cash orders			Total wt. in lbs	
CASH PRICE				
AMOUNT ENCLOSED	Check, Money Order		16 oz. = 1 lb. count any remaining oz. as a full lb.	
	Wards Refund Drafts			

C.O.D. ORDERS Accepted only for phone orders in major cities. See page 935.

HOW WE SHIP . . . Depend on Wards to ship non-mailable items the best way. If you have a preference, please write it here→

REFUNDS by Montgomery Ward are usually made by draft. If a draft is not presented for payment within two years from the date of issue, a service charge thereafter of $1 per year (but not more than the face value of the draft) will be deducted.

C 937

SAMPLE ORDER FORM

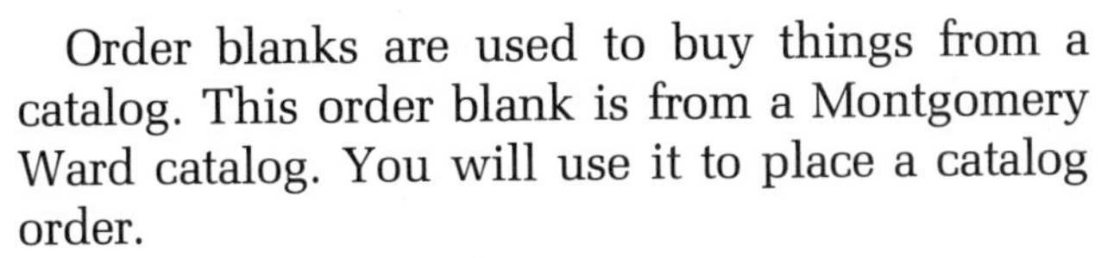

Order blanks are used to buy things from a catalog. This order blank is from a Montgomery Ward catalog. You will use it to place a catalog order.

First, read all the parts of the order blank. These words are important to know.

my present name, address — your name and where you *now* live

method of payment — how you will pay for the things that you order

finance charge — extra cost added to your bill if you do not pay in full when it is due

c.o.d. orders — cash on delivery
A service charge is added if you wait to pay when the items are delivered.

how we ship — how your purchase will be delivered

preference — your choice

refunds — money given back when you return merchandise

draft — a paper which says that a store owes you money. You must cash it in at the store.

On a separate sheet of paper, make the bottom half of the order blank. Choose three items from the sample catalog page that you would like to order. Fill in all the necessary information. When you find your total cost, don't forget the sales tax, if your state has one.

MONEY ORDERS

When paying for something by mail, a money order can be used. It is much safer than putting cash in the envelope, because a money order can only be spent by the person or business whose name is on it. Banks, currency exchanges, post offices, and some retail stores sell money orders. The money order is good for the amount of money that you pay. Sometimes, there is also an extra charge for the service.

SAMPLE FORM

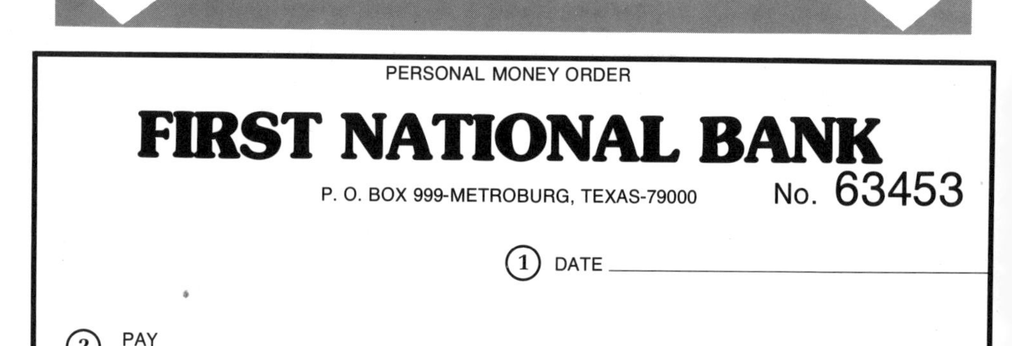

PERSONAL MONEY ORDER

FIRST NATIONAL BANK

P. O. BOX 999-METROBURG, TEXAS-79000 No. 63453

(1) DATE ____________________

(2) PAY TO THE ORDER OF ____________________

(5) NOT VALID OVER $500.00

PERSONAL MONEY ORDER

(3) ____________________ PURCHASER'S SIGNATURE

(4) ____________________ ADDRESS

Suppose you wanted to pay for the merchandise that you ordered from Montgomery Ward with a money order. Do you remember how much your catalog order cost?

On a separate sheet of paper, number from 1 to 5. Fill in the correct information for a money order so that you can pay for your catalog order. For number 5, tell the meaning of "Not valid over $500.00."

AN APPLICATION FOR A SOCIAL SECURITY NUMBER

The government requires that everyone has a social security number before getting a job. When people are employed, a small amount of money is taken out of each paycheck for social security. Older people who no longer work, receive money from the federal government every month.

An application for a social security number can be obtained at a post office. One side of the form has fourteen questions which you must answer. The other side gives you instructions.

SAMPLE FORM

1 *Print* FULL NAME YOU WILL USE IN WORK OR BUSINESS — *(First Name)* *(Middle Name or Initial – if none, draw line___)* *(Last Name)*

2 *Print* FULL NAME GIVEN YOU AT BIRTH

6 YOUR DATE OF BIRTH — *(Month)* *(Day)* *(Year)*

3 PLACE OF BIRTH — *(City)* *(County if known)* *(State)*

7 YOUR PRESENT AGE *(Age on last birthday)*

4 MOTHER'S FULL NAME AT HER BIRTH *(Her maiden name)*

8 YOUR SEX — MALE ☐ FEMALE ☐

5 FATHER'S FULL NAME *(Regardless of whether living or dead)*

9 YOUR COLOR OR RACE — WHITE ☐ NEGRO ☐ OTHER ☐

10 HAVE YOU EVER BEFORE APPLIED FOR OR HAD A UNITED STATES SOCIAL SECURITY, RAILROAD, OR TAX ACCOUNT NUMBER? — NO ☐ DON'T KNOW ☐ YES ☐ *(If "YES" Print STATE in which you applied and DATE you applied and SOCIAL SECURITY NUMBER if known)*

11 YOUR MAILING ADDRESS — *(Number and Street, Apt. No., P.O. Box, or Rural Route)* *(City)* *(State)* *(Zip Code)*

12 TODAY'S DATE

13 TELEPHONE NUMBER

14 NOTICE: Whoever, with intent to falsify his or someone else's true identity, willfully furnishes or causes to be furnished false information in applying for a social security number, is subject to a fine of not more than $1,000 or imprisonment for up to 1 year, or both.

Sign YOUR NAME HERE *(Do Not Print)*

TREASURY DEPARTMENT Internal Revenue Service
FORM SS-5 (5-74)

☐ RESCREEN ☐ ASSIGN ☐ DUP ISSUED

Return completed application to nearest SOCIAL SECURITY ADMINISTRATION OFFICE

First, read the instructions on top of the next page. Then, look at the questions on this form. On a separate sheet of paper, number from one to fourteen. Fill in all the information required on the application. Read the NOTICE by number 14 carefully. This says that you must not use anyone else's name—"falsify his or someone else's true identity." You must fill out the form correctly and truthfully.

INSTRUCTIONS
One Number Is All You Ever Need For Social Security And Tax Purposes
Special Attention Should Be Given To Items Listed Below

Fill in this form completely and correctly. If any information is not known and is unavailable write "unknown" Use typewriter or print legibly in dark ink.

1 Your social security card will be typed with the name you show in item 1. However, if you want to use the name shown in item 2, attach a signed request to this form.

3 If not born in USA, enter the name of the country in which you were born.

5 If a stepfather, adopting father, or foster father is shown, include the relationship after name, for example, "John H. Jones, stepfather."

10 If you have ever before filled out an application like this for a social security, railroad, or tax number, check "yes" even if you never received your card. If you check "yes," give the name of the State and the approximate date on which you applied. Also enter your social security number if you did receive the card and remember the number. You may find your number on an old tax return, payroll slip, or wage statement.

11 If you get your mail in the country, without a street address, show your R.D. Route, and Box number; if at the post office, show your P.O. Box No.; if there is no such way of showing your mail address, show the town or post office name. If mail under your name is not normally received at the address which you show, use an "in care of" address.

14 Sign your name as usually written. Do not print unless this is your usual signature. (If unable to write, make a mark witnessed by two persons who can write. The witnesses preferably should be persons who work with the applicant and both must sign this application. A parent, guardian, or custodian who completes this form on behalf of another person should sign his own name followed by his title or relationship to the applicant, for example, "John Smith, father.")

SAMPLE

BANKING SERVICES

There are many services that banks provide. They provide a safe place for people to keep their money. When money is put in a savings account, it is insured. This means that the bank is responsible for it even if it is lost or stolen. The bank pays interest—a small percentage—on money in a savings account. This is a way that people can earn more money.

Banks use the money to make loans to people who want to buy cars and homes. Then, these people must pay interest to the bank.

Other banking services include providing checking accounts, selling money orders and travelers checks, and renting safety deposit boxes, which are places in a vault or safe where people can keep their valuable possessions.

CHECKING ACCOUNTS

Checking accounts make it easy for people to pay their bills. It is safe to send a check through the mail. Many stores will accept personal checks, so people can buy things without carrying lots of cash.

A checking account works like this. People establish an account and put money into the bank. Then, they can write checks to use the same as cash. The person or business who receives the check takes it to the bank and gets the money.

When we put money into our checking account, we use a checking account deposit slip. Be careful when filling out a deposit slip so that your money will not be lost. Notice the arrow which points to the box for the account number. People write the number given to their account in this box. Sometimes the bank will print this number on your checks. This number tells the bank where the money belongs.

The words **total deposit** in the lower right corner show how much money you put into the bank.

SAMPLE FORM

FIRST NATIONAL BANK

DEPOSIT TICKET

Date ____________, 19 ______

Name ______________________

Address ______________________

City & State ______________________

ACCOUNT NUMBER

CASH		
CHECKS LIST SINGLY • ENDORSE EACH ITEM		
TOTAL		
LESS AMOUNT RECEIVED		
TOTAL DEPOSIT		

On a separate sheet of paper, write the information asked for on the deposit slip. Then, pretend that you wanted to deposit two checks. One is a check from your job for $93.21, and one is an income tax refund of $71.04. You want to take out some money to use when you go shopping. (This is written in the space marked **less amount received**.)

How much cash will you need for shopping?

What is your **total deposit**?

What is the meaning of **endorse each item**?

When using the money in a checking account, a person writes out a personal check. These are the parts of a personal check.

1. Your name and address
2. The check number in the checkbook
3. The date the check is written
4. The name of the person or business to which money is being paid
5. The amount of the check, written in numbers
6. The amount of the check, written in words
7. The name of the bank
8. The signature, written name, of the person writing the check
9. The checking account number
10. MEMO—a reminder of why the check was written

SAMPLE FORM

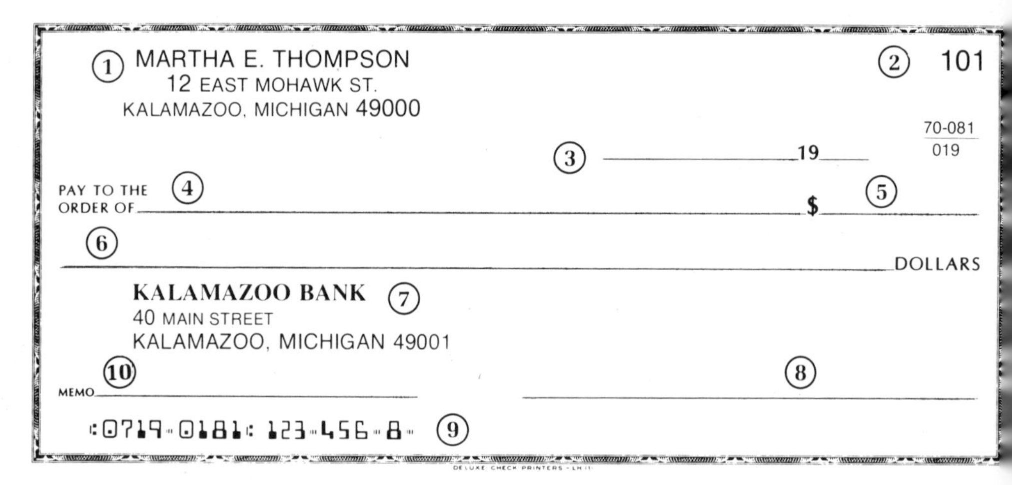

(1) MARTHA E. THOMPSON
12 EAST MOHAWK ST.
KALAMAZOO, MICHIGAN 49000

(2) 101

70-081
019

(3) ______ 19____

PAY TO THE ORDER OF (4) ______ $ (5) ______

(6) ______ DOLLARS

KALAMAZOO BANK (7)
40 MAIN STREET
KALAMAZOO, MICHIGAN 49001

MEMO (10) ______ (8) ______

:0719-0181: 123-456-8- (9)

DELUXE CHECK PRINTERS - LH-II

On a separate sheet of paper, make a check. You want to buy a new shirt which costs $12.60 including the tax. Choose a store where you'd like to buy a shirt. Then, fill in all the needed information on your check.

People must keep an accurate record of how much money they have in their checking accounts. There is a special place in a checkbook to keep this record. People must record each check that they write and each deposit that they make. Look at this sample record.

SAMPLE PAGE

PLEASE BE SURE TO **DEDUCT** ANY PER CHECK CHARGES OR SERVICE CHARGES THAT MAY APPLY TO YOUR ACCOUNT

CHECK NO.	DATE	CHECKS ISSUED TO OR DESCRIPTION OF DEPOSIT	(−) AMOUNT OF CHECK		√ T	(−) CHECK FEE (IF ANY)	(+) AMOUNT OF DEPOSIT		BALANCE	
									63	40
112	9-10	News Agency	6	25					6	25
									57	15
	9-12	Deposit					121	90	121	90
									179	05
113	9-15	Bell Telephone	17	65					17	65
									161	40
114	9-23	Sears & Roebuck	43	00					43	00
									118	40
	9-26	Deposit					103	00	103	00
									221	40
115	9-27	Evergreen Apartment	175	00					175	00
		(Rent)							46	40

CHARGE ACCOUNTS AND CREDIT CARDS

A charge account is another way of buying things. With a charge account, a person does not have to carry lots of money. It also lets people buy things which they might not have the money for right now. Before people can open charge accounts, they must fill out an application for credit. The important information a store will require includes where a person works, if a person has money in the bank, and if the person pays bills on time. The new vocabulary words are important to know. The Credit Application from Carson, Pirie, Scott & Company is on the next two pages.

SAMPLE FORM

PERSONAL DATA

NAME FIRST INITIAL LAST

STREET ADDRESS

CITY STATE ZIP CODE HOW LONG

PREVIOUS ADDRESS

CITY STATE ZIP CODE HOW LONG

RENT ☐ OWN ☐ WITH PARENTS ☐ SINGLE ☐ MARRIED ☐ WIDOWED ☐ NO. OF DEPENDENTS

HOME PHONE AGE SOC. SEC. NO.

SPOUSE'S NAME SPOUSE'S SOC. SEC. NO.

NEAREST RELATIVE, NOT LIVING WITH YOU NAME RELATIONSHIP

ADDRESS CITY STATE ZIP

CREDIT REFERENCES

PREVIOUS CREDIT WITH CARSONS
YES ☐ NO ☐ ACCOUNT NUMBER

LANDLORD OR MORTGAGE HOLDER

ADDRESS

PHONE MONTHLY PAYMENT

BANK CITY ☐ CHECKING ☐ SAVINGS

LOANS OWED TO PURPOSE BALANCE MONTHLY PAYMENTS

1.

2.

MONTHLY CHARGE ACCOUNTS LOCATION ACCT. NO. BALANCE

1.

2.

3.

EMPLOYMENT AND INCOME

PRESENT EMPLOYER			PHONE
ADDRESS		CITY	STATE
POSITION	SALARY		HOW LONG
PREVIOUS EMPLOYER			POSITION
ADDRESS		CITY	STATE
SPOUSE'S EMPLOYER			PHONE
ADDRESS		CITY	STATE
POSITION	SALARY		HOW LONG
SOURCE OF OTHER INCOME	MONTHLY AMOUNT		

SAMPLE FO

CARSON PIRIE SCOTT & CO.
03 429 630 2 3
JAMES SMITH
1001 MAPLE
CENTER CITY
IL 60349

spouse — husband or wife

previous address — where a person lived before his or her current address

widowed — husband or wife is dead

landlord or mortgage holder — the person you rent from or the person or place that holds the mortgage on your home

employer — person or place that you work for

position — job you do

income — money you receive

Bills from charge accounts are sent out every month. If you only pay part of your bill, the store adds an extra cost, called a finance charge.

Read and discuss the Credit Application from Carson, Pirie, Scott & Company. Imagine that you are 21 years old. Do you think you'll be married? Will you have a job? On a separate sheet of paper, complete the credit application as though you were 21 years old. Answer all the questions in terms of what your life might be like then!

PASSPORTS

Today, people travel more than ever before. To travel to some foreign countries, people need a special document which is called a passport. A passport is a small book issued by the government, which gives a person permission to leave the country, visit other countries, and return to the United States.

Some post offices have passport application forms. The form asks many questions about you, because a passport is a special kind of identification card. The questions are grouped into seven sections, **A, B, C, D, E, F,** and **G**. The following words are important to know on a passport application.

Page 1, Section A: approximate date of departure—the date, or as close as possible to the date, that you are planning to leave on your trip.

visible distinguishing marks—any unusual marks on your face or body which can be seen.

Page 2, Section **D:** marriage terminated—divorced

Section **E:** previously married—married before

Section **G:** purpose of trip—reason for your traveling

proposed length of stay—how long you plan to spend traveling

abroad—across the ocean

departure—leaving

On a separate sheet of paper, number from 1 to 4. Answer each question with the capital letter which identifies the section on the passport application form.

1. In what section are the questions about your mother and father?
2. Where do you write where you are going on your trip and how long you plan to stay?
3. Where do you write information about yourself, such as your name and birth date?
4. Where do you give information about a husband or wife and children?

SAMPLE FORM

A

TO BE COMPLETED BY ALL APPLICANTS — **Page 1**

(First name) (Middle name) (Last name)

I, ______________________________

a citizen of the United States, do hereby apply to the Department of State for a passport.

MAIL PASSPORT TO:

IN CARE OF (If applicable) ______________________________

STREET ______________________________

CITY ______________ STATE ______________ ZIP CODE ______________

PHONE NOS. Area Code ________ Home: ______________ Business: ______________

DATE OF BIRTH (Month) (Day) (Year)			PLACE OF BIRTH (City, State or Province, Country)
HEIGHT ______ Ft. ______ In.	COLOR OF HAIR (Spell out)	COLOR OF EYES (Spell out)	APPROXIMATE DATE OF DEPARTURE
VISIBLE DISTINGUISHING MARKS		OCCUPATION	SOCIAL SECURITY NO.
MY PERMANENT RESIDENCE (Street address, City, State, ZIP Code) Phone No.			COUNTY OF RESIDENCE

B

COMPLETE ONLY IF WIFE/HUSBAND OR CHILDREN UNDER THE AGE OF 18 YEARS ARE TO BE INCLUDED IN PASSPORT AND SUBMIT GROUP PHOTOGRAPH

(WIFE'S) (HUSBAND'S) FULL LEGAL NAME

DATE OF BIRTH (Mo., Day, Year)	PLACE OF BIRTH (City, State or Province, Country)	
CHILD(REN) NAME(S) IN FULL	PLACE OF BIRTH (City, State or Country)	DATE OF BIRTH (Month, Day, Year)

C

TO BE COMPLETED BY APPLICANT FOR HIMSELF AND PERSONS INCLUDED

HAVE YOU OR ANYONE INCLUDED IN THIS APPLICATION BEEN ISSUED OR INCLUDED IN A U.S. PASSPORT?
☐ YES ☐ NO (IF YES, GIVE DATE OF MOST RECENT PASSPORT ISSUED AND NAME IN WHICH ISSUED)

IF NOT SUBMITTED WITH THIS APPLICATION:
Where issued:
Disposition:

IN THE EVENT OF ACCIDENT OR DEATH NOTIFY (Do not show name of a person who will accompany you when traveling)
Name in full: Relationship:
Street address, City, State: Phone No.

FORM DSP-11 9-74

D TO BE COMPLETE

FATHER'S NAME	FATHER'S PLAC
MOTHER'S MAIDEN NAME	MOTHER'S PLAC
☐ I WAS NEVER MARRIED ☐ I WAS LAST MARRIED ON	TO (Full legal nar
BORN AT (City, State, Country)	☐ WHO IS A U.S. CITIZEN ☐ WHO IS NOT A U.S. CITIZEN

E WOMEN MUST COMPLETE FOLLOWING IF CHILDREN OF A PREVIO

I WAS PREVIOUSLY MARRIED ON	TO (Full legal name)
ON (Date of birth)	☐ FORMER HUSBAND WAS U.S. CITIZE ☐ FORMER HUSBAND WAS NOT CITIZE

F COMPLETE IF APPLICANT OR ANY PERS

ENTERED THE U.S. (Month) (Year) ☐ APPLICANT ☐ WIFE ☐ HUSBAND ☐ CHILD	IF FATH DATE BEFORE (Name of Court)
RESIDED CONTINUOUSLY IN THE U.S. From (Year) To (Year) ☐ APPLICANT ☐ WIFE ☐ HUSBAND ☐ CHILD	IF MOTH DATE BEFORE (Name of Court)

G PROPOSED TRAVEL PLANS - TO

PURPOSE OF TRIP	MEANS OF TRANSPORTATION SH Departure ☐ Return ☐
PROPOSED LENGTH OF STAY	DO YOU EXPECT TO TAK ☐ Yes ☐ No ☐ Year ☐ 2 Years
NO. OF PREVIOUS TRIPS ABROAD WITHIN LAST 12 MONTHS	

Note: passport application changed slightly to fit the size of the page.

Page 2

ALL APPLICANTS

BIRTH	FATHER'S DATE OF BIRTH	☐ U.S. CITIZEN ☐ NOT U.S. CITIZEN
BIRTH	MOTHER'S DATE OF BIRTH	☐ U.S. CITIZEN ☐ NOT U.S. CITIZEN

omplete whether widowed or divorced) | WHO WAS BORN ON (Date)

☐ MARRIAGE NOT TERMINATED

☐ MARRIAGE TERMINATED BY ☐ Death ☐ Divorce on (Date)

RRIAGE ARE INCLUDED OR IF PREVIOUSLY MARRIED BEFORE MARCH 1931

WHO WAS BORN AT (City, State, Country)

PREVIOUS MARRIAGE TERMINATED BY ☐ DEATH ☐ DIVORCE

ON (Date)

CLUDED WAS NOT BORN IN THE UNITED STATES

ATURALIZED:	IF KNOWN, FATHER'S RESIDENCE IN U.S. From (Year) To (Year)
CERTIFICATE NO.	
PLACE (City, State)	

ATURALIZED:	IF KNOWN, MOTHER'S RESIDENCE IN U.S. From (Year) To (Year)
CERTIFICATE NO.	
PLACE (City, State)	

PLETED BY ALL APPLICANTS

Air	Other	COUNTRIES TO BE VISITED
☐	☐	
☐	☐	

HER TRIP ABROAD?

O, WITHIN

☐ 5 Years

UNEMPLOYMENT COMPENSATION

Sometimes, people lose their jobs and are unable to find new jobs right away. When people are unemployed, they can often receive money from their state government. Money paid to people who are out of work, in order to make up for lost wages, is called **unemployment compensation**. The questions are not difficult to understand. They must be answered carefully and honestly. Mistakes could cause delays in the payment of money.

Notice that every question on this form has a number. These words are important to know.

9. **lack of work** — the business did not have work for you to do and could not pay you

17. **refused any offers of work** turned down a job

18. **dismissal** — being fired from a job
    bonus pay — extra money besides your regular salary
    pension — money paid to a person who retires from a business

19. **step-children** — children born to a wife or husband in a previous marriage
    legally adopted children — giving one's name and care to children through a court procedure
    disability — something which is wrong, either physically or mentally
    consecutive days — days in a row, or following one after another
    immediately preceding — right before

20. **prescribes penalities** — gives punishment

On a separate sheet of paper, number from 1 to 21. Answer all the questions on the claim for unemployment compensation.

SAMPLE FORM

ENTER SOCIAL SECURITY NUMBER HERE → 1. SOCIAL SECURITY NUMBER

2. FIRST NAME | MIDDLE NAME | LAST NAME

FOR OFFICE USE ONLY

DATE OF CLAIM	D.C.	L. O. #	IT.PT.
BASE PERIOD ENDS QTR. YR.	R & S	BEN. YR. BEGINS	
DATE ISSUED		BEN. YR. ENDS	

REMARKS

3. STREET ADDRESS

8. OTHER NAMES OR SOCIAL SECURITY NUMBERS USED, IF ANY

4. CITY OR TOWN | 5. STATE | 6. ZIP CODE | 7. YEAR OF BIRTH

9. I LOST MY LAST JOB BECAUSE OF (CHECK ONE) → ☐ LACK OF WORK ☐ OTHER REASON (EXPLAIN) →

10. LAST DAY WORKED — MONTH DAY YEAR

11. FIRM NAME OF LAST EMPLOYER →

BEN-224 ISSUED — S. S. NO. VERIFIED ☐

12. STREET ADDRESS OF EMPLOYER →

DATE CLAIM ACCEPTED ____

DATE BEN-30 SENT C.O. ____

CHECK WAGE RECORDS OF SPOUSE ☐

13. CITY OR TOWN → | 14. STATE | 15. ZIP CODE

WORK HISTORY

FROM ____ TO ____ EARNED ____

FROM ____ TO ____ EARNED ____

FROM ____ TO ____ EARNED ____

SIGNATURE OF CLAIMS TAKER

16. I LAST FILED A CLAIM FOR UNEMPLOYMENT COMPENSATION AGAINST THE STATE OF ____ IN THE MONTH OF ____ YEAR ____

DURING THE PAST TWO YEARS I HAVE { WORKED OUTSIDE ILLINOIS — YES OR NO ☐; WORKED FOR THE FEDERAL GOVERNMENT — YES OR NO ☐; SERVED IN THE U. S. ARMED FORCES — YES OR NO ☐ }

17. HAVE YOU REFUSED ANY OFFERS OF WORK SINCE YOU BECAME UNEMPLOYED?................(Yes or No)

18. DID YOU RECEIVE OR WILL YOU BE PAID MONEY FOR ANY PERIOD AFTER THE LAST DAY YOU WORKED (DISMISSAL, VACATION, OR BONUS PAY OR A PRIVATE RETIREMENT PENSION PAID FOR IN FULL OR IN PART BY A FORMER EMPLOYER)?..........(Yes or No)

19. COMPLETE THIS SECTION IF YOU HAVE A DEPENDENT CHILD (OR CHILDREN).

If you have any children, including step-children and legally adopted children, under 18 years of age (or older, if unable to work for the past 90 days, because of illness or other disability), enter below the names, addresses, and birthdates of not more than 4 of them.

Name	Address	Birth Date
(1) Name	Address	Birth Date
(2) Name	Address	Birth Date
(3) Name	Address	Birth Date
(4) Name	Address	Birth Date

a. Is any other person claiming any of the above children as a dependent on an Illinois claim?..........(Yes or No)

b. Did you furnish more than one-half the cost of the support of the children listed above for at least 90 consecutive days immediately preceding the date of this claim?..........(Yes or No)

20. COMPLETE THIS SECTION IF YOU HAVE NO DEPENDENT CHILDREN BUT DO HAVE A DEPENDENT WIFE (OR HUSBAND)

Wife's (or Husband's) Name	Address (if different from yours)	Her (or His) Social Security #

a. Did you furnish more than one-half the cost of the support for your lawful wife (or husband) for at least 90 consecutive days immediately preceding the date of this claim?..........(Yes or No)

b. Did your wife (or husband) work in Illinois within the past 2 years?..........(Yes or No)

21. CERTIFICATION: I hereby register for work and file a claim for unemployment compensation benefits. I certify that all the information submitted on this claim is true and correct to the best of my knowledge and belief. I AM AWARE THAT THE LAW PRESCRIBES PENALTIES OF FINE AND IMPRISONMENT FOR MAKING ANY FALSE STATEMENTS TO OBTAIN BENEFITS.

UC (ILL.) BEN-32 (REV. 1-75)

CLAIM RECORD CARD

CLAIMANT'S SIGNATURE ____ (WRITE YOUR NAME - DO NOT PRINT) ____ (DATE)

SAMPLE FORM

PUBLIC AID

Sometimes, people need some special help to take care of themselves. Sometimes, they have problems which they cannot handle alone. They can ask their state government for money and medical care. People can apply for public aid at special offices throughout their state.

This application form requests help for the aged, blind, or disabled from the Illinois Department of Public Aid. People who cannot take care of themselves and are over age 65, blind, or have some mental or physical disability, would use this form. These are some important words to know:

4. disabled ——— a mental or physical handicap which prevents a person from working
5. emergency ——— a serious problem needing immediate help
6. living costs——— the money needed to support oneself to stay alive
8. food stamps ——— a kind of help which lets people buy food at a cheaper price
17. social security money taken from your paycheck by the government, which is paid to retired and disabled people. (You already filled out the application for a social security number!)
19. Medicare——— a kind of health insurance
21. railroad retirement ——— money for people who worked on railroads
25. deceased——— dead
27. landlord ——— a person who owns a building and rents out rooms or apartments to people
29. mortgage——— money owed on a house or property

SAMPLE FORM

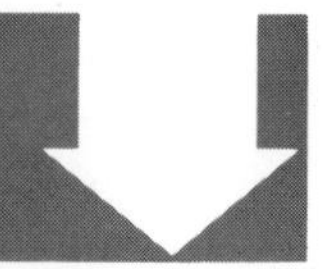

For Office Use Only

Date given the Applicant: ______ Category: ______ Case Number: ______

Illinois Department of Public Aid

Request for Public Aid for The Aged, Blind, or Disabled

Please answer all questions. Your answers should be about the person who needs aid. If you need help in completing this application, ask for it.

1. What is your Name and Address?

☐ Mr. ☐ Mrs. ☐ Miss

______
Last Name | First Name | Middle Name | Maiden Name

______
Street Address or Rural Route | Apartment and Floor or Box Number | City or Town | State | Zip Code

2. What's Your Telephone Number?

____ — ____ — ____
Area Code

3. If you do not have a Telephone, is there a number where you can be reached?

If you cannot be reached by telephone, write "none."

____ — ____ — ____
Area Code

4. Why are you applying for Aid?

☐ Are you 65 or older?
☐ Are you blind, or do you see very poorly?
☐ Do you have a serious health problem? What? ______

☐ Are you disabled? How? ______
☐ Explain any other reason you can't work. ______

What Kind of Help do You Need?

5. Do you need Emergency Help?

☐ Money
☐ Food
☐ Clothes
☐ A Place to Live
Explain any other Help You need ______

6. Do you need help with Living Costs?

☐ Medical bills
☐ Furniture
☐ Bills you can't pay
For what? ______

7. Do you need help paying Medical bills only?

☐ Yes ☐ No

8. Do you need help buying more food with FOOD STAMPS?

☐ Yes ☐ No

9. Do you need help with other problems you have?

☐ Poor health
☐ Special diet prescribed by Doctor
☐ Going into a Hospital or home where you can get special care
☐ Caring for yourself
Are you unable to get out of your bed or a chair without help?
☐ Yes ☐ No

☐ Caring for your home
Does someone live with you, or come in, to help you care for yourself or your home?
☐ Yes ☐ No
☐ Someone to go shopping, do chores, or run errands
☐ Buying extra-large clothes, or special shoes

☐ Getting Job Training or Adult Education
☐ Getting to and from the Doctor's Office, Hospital or Clinic
☐ Having a baby. When? ______
☐ Explain any other problems you have ______

10. How have you been paying for your living expenses for the past month?

______

11. Have you ever gotten Public Aid, Welfare, or Relief before?

☐ Yes ☐ No
What was your name then? ______
When? ______
Where? ______ County ______ State ______

DPA 560 (R-12-71)

27. Where do you live?

Check the proper box

☐ A Rented Apartment, House, or Trailer
Does the Landlord provide the Furniture you use?
☐ Yes ☐ No
☐ A Chicago Housing Authority Apartment

☐ Other Public Housing
☐ Your own Home or Trailer
☐ Another Person's Home
☐ A Boarding House
☐ A Hotel
☐ A Hospital or Care Home
What is its Name?

☐ Another kind of Housing (What kind?)
____
____

28. How many Rooms do you live in?

(Do not count Bathroom)

Number of Rooms ________

29. What are your Living Costs?

	AMOUNT PAID	HOW OFTEN IS IT DUE?	Is it Paid up to date?
☐ Rent	$		☐ Yes ☐ No
☐ Mortgage Payment	$		☐ Yes ☐ No
If your home has a Co-Owner, what is his name? ...			
☐ Taxes, above the Mortgage ..	$		☐ Yes ☐ No
☐ Insurance, above the Mortgage	$		☐ Yes ☐ No
☐ Trailer Lot or Parking	$		☐ Yes ☐ No
☐ Garbage or Trash Pickup ...	$		☐ Yes ☐ No
☐ Water	$		☐ Yes ☐ No
☐ Sewer	$		☐ Yes ☐ No

30. Check the Utilities you also pay for

	Is it Paid up to date?
Electricity	☐ Yes ☐ No
Heating Fuel (What Kind) ________	☐ Yes ☐ No
Cooking Fuel	☐ Yes ☐ No

31. Do you pay to do your Laundry?

☐ Yes ☐ No

32. List Everyone Who Lives With You

Do not answer this question if you live in a Hotel, Boarding House, Hospital or any sort of Care Home.

NAME	His or Her Relation to you	Does He or She get Public Aid?
1.		☐ Yes ☐ No
2.		☐ Yes ☐ No
3.		☐ Yes ☐ No
4.		☐ Yes ☐ No
5.		☐ Yes ☐ No
6.		☐ Yes ☐ No

33. How many people eat together where you live?

Number ________

34. Check box below if you must eat some of your meals in a Restaurant or have them brought to your home.

Which meals are these?

☐ Breakfast ☐ Noon Meal ☐ Evening Meal

DPA 560 (R-12-71)

SAMPLE FORM

35. If you own any of the things listed below, please show their value

Do you, or does your husband or wife, own any of these things?		Write Value here: Yours	Your Husband or Wife's
Land or buildings you don't live in..	(Sale Value)	$	
Life Insurance	(Face Value)	$	
Health Insurance	(Company)		
Money in a Savings or Checking Account	(Amount)	$	
Cash on Hand	(Amount)	$	
Stocks or Bonds	(Cash Value)	$	
Prepaid Burial Plan	(Cash Value)	$	
Do you also have a Burial Lot? ...	☐ Yes ☐ No	$	
Anything else Valuable	(Value)	$	

What is it? ______

36. Have you Sold or Transferred any Property in the last 5 years?

This includes a house, land, any real estate, stocks or bonds or any other valuables.

☐ Yes ☐ No If Yes, please answer the following:

What was the Date of Sale or Transfer? ______

How much were you paid? ______

Was it a Fair Price? ______

Why did you Sell or Transfer this Property? ______

37. Do You, Or Does Your Husband Or Wife, Get Money From Any Of The Following Sources?

	Yours	How Often Do You Get It?	Your Husband Or Wife's	How Often Does He Or She Get It?
Social Security	$		$	
Railroad Retirement	$		$	
Veteran's Pension	$		$	
Any Other Pension	$		$	
Insurance, Including Railroad Unemployment And Workman's Compensation	$		$	
Unemployment Compensation Benefits	$		$	
Any Sick Benefits	$		$	
Total Earnings From *Any Work Or Training*	$		$	
Public Aid, Welfare, Or Relief	$		$	
Payments Received From A Roomer, Boarder, Or Property	$		$	
Any Other Income	$		$	
Money Or Help Received From A Friend or Relative. If Not Money, What? ______	$		$	

38. If You Or Your Husband Or Wife Have Any Income, List Your Deductions And Your Work Expenses.

Answer This Question If You Listed Earnings Above.	Your Work	Your Husband Or Wife's Work
Income Tax Deductions	$	$
Social Security	$	$
Group Life Insurance	$	$
Medical Or Hospitalization Insurance	$	$
Pension Or Retirement Fund	$	$
Credit Union Deductions	$	$
Union Dues	$	$

Do You Buy Your Lunches At Work? .... ☐ Yes ☐ No

Do You Take Your Lunch To Work? .... ☐ Yes ☐ No

Do You Pay For Uniforms Or Special Tools? .... ☐ Yes ☐ No

How Do You Get To And From Work? ______

DPA 560 (R-12-71)

SAMPLE FORM

This Section Tells About Your Background

12. When were you born?

Month Day Year

13. What State (or Foreign Country) were you born in?

14. Where did you live before you came to Illinois?

15. When did you move to Illinois?

Month Year

16. What Race are you?

17. What is your Social Security Account Number?

Copy your Number from your Social Security Card.

18. What is your Social Security Claim Number?

Copy your Claim Number from your Social Security check, if you get one.

19. What is your Medicare Claim Number?

Copy your Claim Number from your Medicare (Health Insurance) Card, if you have one.

20. If you do not get a Social Security check, have you applied for Social Security benefits?

☐ Yes. ☐ No

When? ______

21. What is your Railroad Retirement Account Number?

Copy your Account Number from your Railroad Retirement Card, if you have one.

22. What is your Railroad Retirement Claim Number?

Copy your Claim Number from your Railroad Retirement Check, if you have one.

23. Have you ever been Married?

☐ Yes ☐ No

If Yes, are you now . . .

☐ Married, and presently living together
☐ Legally Separated by a Court Order
☐ Separated without a Court Order
☐ Married, but not able to live together
☐ Widowed
☐ Divorced

Why? ______

24. What is your Husband or Wife's Name and Address?

Name ______

Street Address or Rural Route

Apartment and Floor or Box Number

City or Town

State or Country

25. Have you, or has someone in your Family, born in the United States Armed Forces?

☐ Yes ☐ No

If Yes, Who?

☐ Yourself
☐ Your Husband or Wife
☐ Your deceased Husband or Wife
☐ Your Parents or Children. Who?

Name Relation to you

Name Relation to you

26. If there is an Accident or Emergency, who should the Public Aid Office call?

Name Relation to you

Street Address or Rural Route

Apartment and Floor or Box Number

City or Town

State

Telephone Number ______

DPA 560 (R-12-71)

SAMPLE FORM

30. utilities ——— public services such as gas, water, and electricity

37. pension ——— money paid to a person who has retired from a business

veteran ——— a person who has served in one of the armed forces of the United States

unemployment compensation— money paid to people who are out of work and cannot find jobs

roomer ——— a person who rents a room in a house

boarder ——— a person who pays money for a room and meals in a home

38. deductions ——— money which is taken out of every paycheck for a special purpose

If you had a grandmother who needed help, you could help her fill out this form. Write the letters A to E down the left side of a separate sheet of paper. Then, write the number of the question of the form which asks you for the following information.

A. why you need aid

B. the people you live with

C. when you were born

D. if you are married

E. if you need someone to go shopping or do chores for you

FORMS

Some people feel nervous when they are asked to fill out a form. In this chapter, we have looked at many different kinds of forms. Many of the forms have asked for the same information. They were not difficult to understand.

Always remember to read a form *before* writing on it. Be sure to understand what the question is asking *before* you try to answer it. Now, you should be ready to fill out any form correctly.

Chapter TWELVE

WHAT DO I KNOW ABOUT USING THE LIBRARY?

A library is different things to different people. For some people, it is a place to find books which they enjoy reading. Mysteries, love stories, and sports are topics that many people like. For some people, the library is a place to explore and discover new things. Encyclopedias and other reference books are filled with exciting information. Libraries also have records, magazines, and newspapers. Some people use the newspapers when they're looking for a job.

There is so much a person can discover in a library. All libraries are arranged in the same way. If you learn your way around your school library, you will be able to use any library.

FICTION BOOKS

Fiction books are novels and stories made up by the author. These books are arranged on shelves in alphabetical order according to the authors' last names.

The following are titles of books and the authors' names. On a separate sheet of paper, rewrite this list and put the books in alphabetical order according to the authors' last names. Your new list will show the order that the books would be found on the shelves in the library.

Around the World in Eighty Days	Jules Verne
Little Women	Louisa May Alcott
Kidnapped	Robert Louis Stevenson
The Call of the Wild	Jack London
The Good Earth	Pearl S. Buck
First Jungle Book	Rudyard Kipling
Lost Horizon	James Hilton
Oliver Twist	Charles Dickens
Tom Sawyer	Mark Twain

NONFICTION BOOKS

Nonfiction books contain facts and information. These books are divided into ten number groups known as the Dewey Decimal System. Books are arranged on the shelves by numbers which are clearly seen on the backs of the books as they stand upright on the shelves. There are letters under each number which are the first two letters of the author's last name. The number, together with the two letters, is known as the **call number**. This number helps locate the book on the shelf. Books about the same subject are given the same number group and placed together on the shelf. This basic grouping of books in all libraries is listed below.

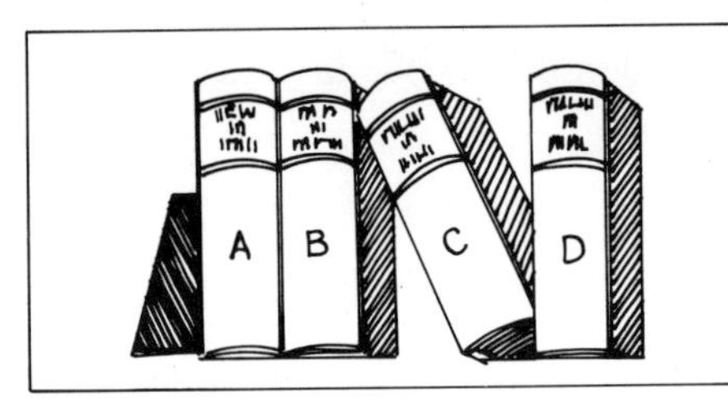

000-099:
All reference books (encyclopedias, almanacs, and bibliographies)

100-199:
Philosophy (man's mind and thoughts)

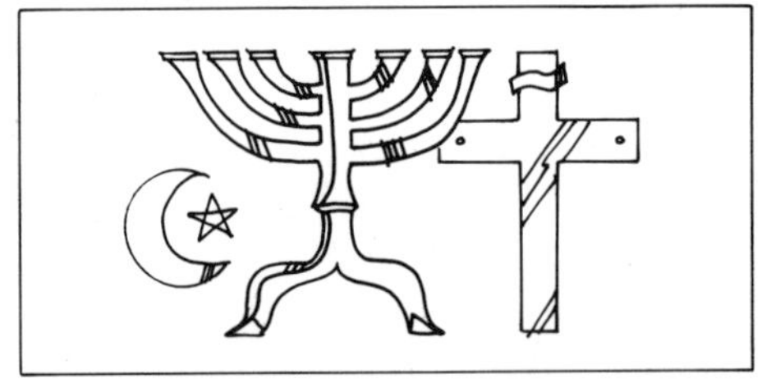

200-299:
Religion

300-399:
Social Sciences (government, law)

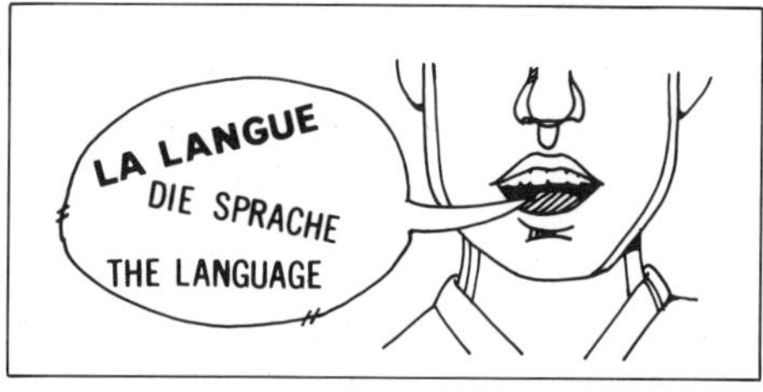

400-499:
Languages

500-599:
Science (math, chemistry, physics)

600-699:
Applied Science, Useful Arts (medicine, engineering, invention)

700-799:
Fine Arts and Recreation (painting, drawing, sculpture, music, dance, theatre, sports, games)

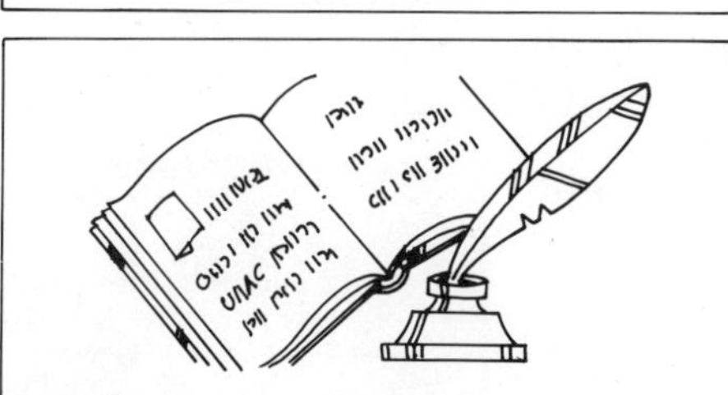

800-899:
Literature (novels, plays, poetry)

900-999:
History, Biography, Geography, Travel

Which number group in the Dewey Decimal System contains books on the following subjects? Check with the list. Write your answers on a separate sheet of paper.

1. The Bible
2. The Atomic Bomb
3. The History of Painting
4. A Trip to Mexico
5. Heart Surgery
6. The Life Story of Benjamin Franklin
7. The History of the Movies
8. Democracy in America
9. How to Speak Spanish
10. The Tragic Play of "Romeo and Juliet"

CARD CATALOG

The card catalog is an index of all the books in the library. It is a cabinet with many small drawers which are labeled with the letters A to Z.

Some drawers have more than one letter on the label. All libraries have a card catalog, but not all card catalogs have the same letter groups on each drawer. This illustration is an example of how letters are grouped on a card catalog.

For each book, there are three cards in the card catalog. The **subject card** has the subject or topic of the book written at the top of the card. The **title card** has the title or name of the book across the top. Note: if the first word of a title is *A, An,* or *The,* the card for the book is filed by the second word in the title. The **author card** has the author's name at the top, with the last name written first.

All cards have the call number of the book in the upper left corner. To find the book on the shelves, locate the number group and then look for the specific number and the author's initial which make up the call number.

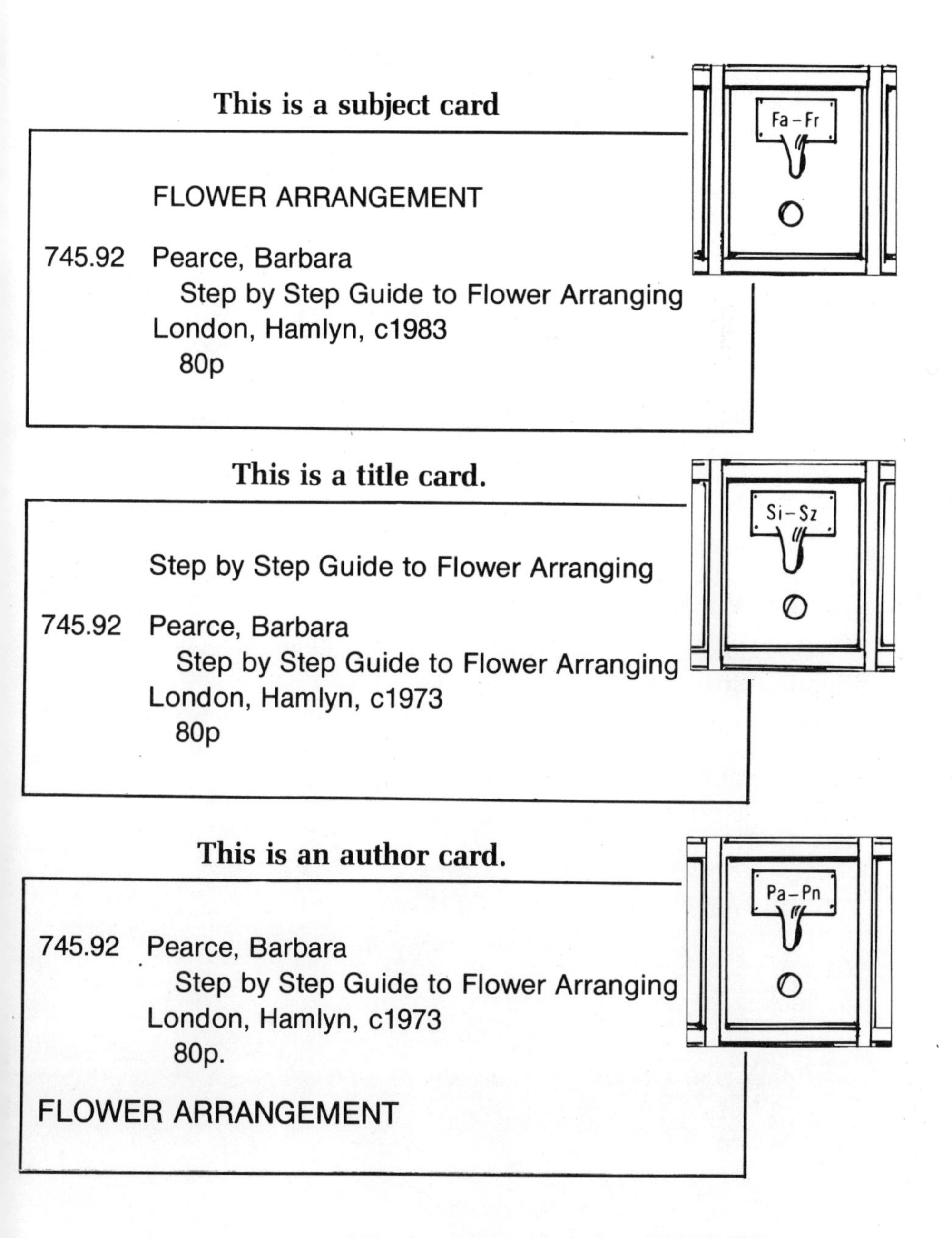

AUTHOR CARDS

The following authors have cards in the card catalog of your school library. Look in the card catalog and find the *author card* for each of the names. On a separate sheet of paper, list a title of one of the books which each author has written. Remember, author cards are always filed by the author's *last* name.

F. L. Allen	Robert Frost
Charles Schulz	E. E. Cummings
John B. Anderson	William Shakespeare
R. E. Church	Samuel Clemens
Janet Spencer	Sarah Teasdale
Alfred Church	Elizabeth Barrett Browning
Robert Baker	Robert Browning
Carl Sandburg	Edgar Allan Poe

TITLE CARDS

On a separate sheet of paper, write the following book titles in alphabetical order.

Edith Wharton by Irving Howe
The Married Look by Nathan Robert
The Sea Wolf by Jack London
A Boy to Remember by Amelia Elizabeth
An American Girl by Patricia Dizen
How to Bring Up Your Pet Dog by Kurt Unkelboch
One Summer by Mary Levin
A Holiday With Eric by Ruth Dagget Leinhuaser
Sport, Sport, Sport by John Lowell Pratt
The F.B.I. by James Quentin Reynolds

SUBJECT CARDS

Do this activity in your school library. Which drawers in the card catalog have cards for the books on the following subjects? On a separate sheet of paper, write the letter or letters shown on the outside of the drawer in which you find each subject.

1. automobile repair	6. Marie Sklodowska Curie
2. boats	7. pollution
3. diets	8. macrame
4. cancer	9. Baseball Hall of Fame
5. hockey	10. vocational education

Using the Card Catalog

Do this activity in your school library. Which drawers in the card catalog have cards for the books written by the following authors? On a separate sheet of paper, write the letter or letters shown on the outside of the drawer in which you find each author's name.

1. Lincoln Stephens
2. Sylvia Plath
3. Edgar Allen Poe
4. Carl Sandburg
5. Margaret Mead

Which drawers in the card catalog have cards for the following book titles? On a separate sheet of paper, write the letters or letters shown on the outside of the drawer in which you find each book title.

1. The American Woman by Mark Louis McBee
2. Famous Negro Entertainers On Stage, Screen and TV by Charlemae Rollins
3. Wonderful World of the Automobile by Ken W. Purdy
4. Vacationland U.S.A. by National Geographic Magazine
5. Fahrenheit 451 by Ray Bradbury

REFERENCE BOOKS

ENCYCLOPEDIAS

Encyclopedias are used frequently by many people. *The Encyclopedia Britannica, The World Book Encyclopedia,* and *Compton's Picture Encyclopedia* are usually found on special shelves in almost every school library. These books tell us about people, places, things, and happenings all over the world. Generally, all articles in the encyclopedia are arranged alphabetically. There is a guide word at the top of each page to help us find the titles and the subjects of the articles on the page. Subjects that begin with the letter A are in Volume A. Subjects that start with the letter B are in Volume B. The letter of the volume is in large print on the back of the volume as it stands upright on the shelf.

Use *The World Book Encyclopedia* in your school library. On a separate sheet of paper, write the volume letter, the volume number, and the page where the following subjects are found.

1. Rockets
2. Money
3. Careers
4. Sports
5. Woman
6. Drugs
7. Doctors
8. Gardening
9. Transportation
10. Joseph Stalin
11. Viet Nam War
12. Olympic Games

THE WORLD ALMANAC

The World Almanac and Book of Facts is another useful book for finding specific facts or details. All the information is updated each year. In front of the book is the General Index. The main headings or subjects are in heavy type. Look for a subject alphabetically.

The main headings of several articles are shown in heavy type below. On a separate sheet of paper, write the answer to each question, using *The World Almanac and Book of Facts* of the current year. Give the page number in the *Almanac* where you found the answer.

1. Look under the heading **Aircraft** (Disasters). What is the total number of people who were killed in airplane crashes in 1973?
2. Look under the heading **Alaska** (Population). What was the population of Anchorage, Alaska, in 1970?
3. Look under the heading **Football** (Pro Football Attendance). Find the year there was a record attendance of people at professional football games. How many people attended?
4. Look under the heading **World War II** (Atomic Bomb). When and where did the United States drop the first atomic bomb?
5. Look under the heading **Kennedy, John F.** (Assassination). When and where was President Kennedy assassinated?
6. Look under the heading **Pulitzer Prizes**. How often is this prize awarded? Who gets the prizes? For whom is the Pulitzer Prize named?
7. Look under the heading **King** (Dr. Martin Luther). Where and on what date was Dr. Martin Luther King assassinated? How old was he?
8. Look under the heading **Salaries** (President of the United States). What is the current salary of the President of the United States?
9. Look under the heading **Ali** (Muhammad). What other name has Ali used? Why did he lose his heavy weight boxing crown in 1967?
10. Look under the heading **Marine Corps U.S.** (Women's Branch). At the present time how many women are in the U.S. Marine Corps?

MAGAZINES

Magazines of all kinds are kept in a library. Some kinds of magazines include sports, fishing, cars, hobbies, crafts, music, gardening, beauty, fashions, business, and jobs. There are news magazines, too. Some magazines are for teenagers and some are for adults. There are many magazines for homemakers.

Magazines are published at regular time periods—every week, month, or several times a year. They are called periodical literature. Magazines have the most recent and up-to-date facts on many subjects. The best way to find a magazine with specific information is to look in the *Readers' Guide to Periodical Literature*. General topics and the names of persons who have written articles are listed alphabetically. There are over 160 magazines whose articles are indexed in the *Readers' Guide*. Each library has a list of the magazines which it has kept for one, two, three, and even five years. There usually isn't enough space in the library to keep magazines for more than five years.

Look at the sample page from the *Readers' Guide*. Under the general subject of "Beatles", four articles are listed that have been written in different magazines. Here is one of the articles listed with each part explained:

1. title of article
2. author of article
3. title of magazine
4. volume of magazine
5. pages
6. date of magazine

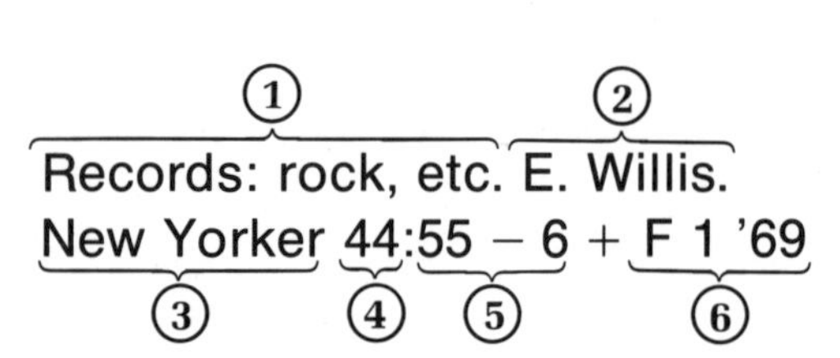

Special abbreviations used by the *Readers' Guide* for listing the months of the year and the names of the magazines are listed in the front of the book.

Sample Entries from Readers' Guide

BEANS
Scarlet runners, a heroic harvest. il Sunset 142: 228+ Mr '69
BEAR claws. See Pastry
BEAR hunting
Bears I have known. B. Cheff. il Outdoor Life 143: 48-51+ F '69
Spring bear hunt. J. W. Valentine. il Outdoor Life 143:78-9+ Mr '69
BEARDWOOD, Roger
Sophistication comes to the tax havens. Fortune 79:94-7+ F '69
BEATLES
Apple corps four. C. E. Fager. Chr Cent 86:386-8 Mr 19 '69
Beatles' ninety-minute bore, and the Rolling Stones'Beggars banquet. J. Gabree. il pors Hi Fi 19:84-5 Mr '69
Records: rock, etc. E. Willis. New Yorker 44:55-6+ F 1 '69
Wisdom of their years. A. G. Aronowitz. Life 66:12 Ja 31 '69
CITIES in Bezique; drama. See Kennedy, A.
CLEMENS, Samuel Langhorne
Man that corrupted Hadleyburg; dramatization. See Nolan, P. T.
about
Never the Twain shall meet. D. Grumbach. Commonweal 89:616-18 F 14 '69
COME along with me; story. See Jackson, S.
COME summer; musical comedy. See Musical comedies, revues, etc.—Criticisms, plots, etc.
COMEDY
Theory of comedy, by E. Olson. Review.
New Repub 160:23-4+ Mr 15 '69. K. Burke
COMIC strips. See Comics (books, strips, etc)
COMICS (books, strips, etc)
Not-so Peanuts world of Charles M. Schulz. J. Tebbel; C. M. Schulz. il Sat R 52:72-4+ Ap 12 '69
DONIZETTI, Gaetano
Lucia di Lammermoor. Criticism
Opera N il por 33:17-20 F 1 '69

FIFTEENTH century
Fifteenth century: the prospect of Europe, by M. Aston. Review
Nat R 21:185-6 F 25 '69. P. P. Wintonski
GUIDEBOOKS
Guide lines to Temple Fielding. N. Busch. il Travel 131:69-72 Mr '69
Inside Paris; A Parisian's guide to Paris, by Henri Gault and Christian Millau. Newsweek 73:100+ Mr 17 '69
Anecdotes, facetiae, satire, etc.
Kentucky on $5 a day. D. Lowe. il Ewquire 71:88+ mr '69
HOCKEY
Found a native who outplays the imports: Boston college's T. Sheehy. M. Mulvoy. il Sports Illus 30:38+ Ja 20 '69
Power play: Russian hockey team tour of Canada. Newsweek 73:58 F 3 '69
Russians lose a pair; and set off 100,000 Czechs. il Life 66:93-4 Ap 11 '69
Some pros go back to college; Denver wins the NCAA championship. G. Ronbeg. il Sports Illus 30:56-7 Mr 24 '69
HOCKEY players
Icy love-in with the red-hot Blues; Stanley cup playoffs. G. Ronberg. il Sports Illus 30:52-4+ Ap 7 '69
It's Bobby Orr & the animals: Bruins a threat to Montreal's reign. M. Mulvoy. il Sports Illus 30: 18-23 F 3 '69
Some pros go back to college; Denver wins the NCAA championship. G. Ronberg. il Sports Illus 30:56-7 Mr 24 '69
Sporting scene; St. Louis Blues success story. H. W. Wind. New Yorker 45:138+ Mr 15 '69
IN the matter of J. Robert Oppenheimer; drama. See Kipphardt, H.
INHERITANCE tax
Estate tax changes coming. il U S News 66:72-4 Ap 7 '69

Look at the sample page, and on a separate sheet of paper, answer the following questions.

Under the subject of BEAR hunting, the article "Bears I Have Known" is listed.

1. Who is the author?
2. In what magazine can you find this article?
3. What is the number of the volume?
4. On what page of the magazine would you find the article?
5. What is the date of the magazine?

Under the subject HOCKEY players, this article is listed, "Some pros go back to college; Denver wins the NCAA championship". Answer the same five questions.

Chapter THIRTEEN

DO I KNOW HOW TO READ THE NEWSPAPER?

Did you hear about the plane crash yesterday?
What happened in the bank robbery?
How many people were killed in the earthquake in Peru?

THE NEWS STORY

The most important job of the newspaper is reporting news from all over the world. People like to know what is happening. Reading the newspaper is a daily habit for many people.

The front page brings us a whole world of happenings. The large black letters across the top announce the biggest news of the day. This is called the *headline.* A news article gives all the details.

A complete news story is usually as short as possible while telling all the important details. A news story will answer these questions: "who?" "what?" "where?" "when?" "why?". The dateline at the beginning of an article often answers the "where" question. The dateline tells the date and place where a news story was written.

This is a sample news article. As you read it, think about the five "w" questions listed above.

Youth Found Under Ice

Boston, Massachusetts, Feb. 17—The search finally ended at 11:00 last night for ten-year-old Bobby Sylvester who had slipped into the icy water while skating on Jamaica Pond earlier in the afternoon. His friend, Joseph Ryan, had tried to pull him out but his efforts failed. According to police, the two boys had failed to observe the "THIN ICE" sign. Bobby Sylvester is survived by his parents, Mr. and Mrs. Jonathon Sylvester, of 443 W. Wrightwood Street, Boston, Massachusetts.

On a separate sheet of paper, write the answers to the following questions about the news article.

1. Look at the dateline. In what city was the story written?
2. WHO are the people in the story?
3. WHAT happened that made this story news?
4. WHERE did the event happen?
5. WHEN did the event in the story take place?
6. WHY did this event happen?

Sometimes, a news story is very long and will continue on another page. Then, there are directions so people can find the rest of the story. These directions might say, "continued on page 4, column 3" or "continued on back page this section."

THE INDEX

Some people don't read the entire newspaper. Some read only their favorite sections. Some readers turn at once to the Sports Section. Others turn to the Financial or Business Section first, because they are interested in business news. Those who are job hunting will check the want ads or classified ads for job openings. Many people like to read the daily happenings in their favorite comic strips.

Every newspaper organizes the sections in a definite pattern. The index to a newspaper is usually on page 2. The index lists all the sections of the paper alphabetically. Readers can use the index to quickly find the location of the section of interest to them.

Look at this index to a newspaper. On a separate sheet of paper, write the section and page number which answer each of the questions that follow.

Index

	Sec.	Pg.		Sec.	Pg.
Action Line	3	1	Living Faith	4	15
Casey Banas	3	2	Jack Mabley	1	4
Bridge	4	6-8	Bob Markus	6	4
Joyce Brothers	4	4	Mary McGory	3	4
Business	7	6	Money Scene	6	9
Business Ticker	6	9	Movies	4	3
Classified	8	7	Music	4	5
Comics	4	7-8	Obituaries	4	14
Crossword Puzzle	4	7	Perspective	3	4
Dear Abby	4	4	Sam Shulsky	6	13
Gary Deeb	4	10	Sports	10	6
Editorials	3	2	Frank Starr	3	2
Harold Finley	6	10	Wayne Stayskal	3	2
Food	4	6	Jerald terHorat	3	4
Horoscope	4	7	Tempo	9	4
How to Keep Well	4	3	Tower Ticker	4	2
John Husar	6	3	Traveler's Guide	4	12
Vernon Jarrett	3	4	TV and Radio	4-9	11
George Lazarus	6	12	Wake of the News	6	3
Dick Locher	3	4	Weather	4	15

1. Where can you find the weather forecast?
2. Where are the comics?
3. Which section contains the classified ads?
4. Where are the obituary reports of the people who have died?
5. Where is the editorial page?
6. Where can you find the score of the game between the Chicago White Sox and the Cleveland Indians?

Now that you can find your way around a newspaper, let's take a closer look at what's inside some important sections of a newspaper.

AMUSEMENTS / ENTERTAINMENT

The Amusements or Entertainment Section helps people find fun things to do in their free time. Here, anyone can discover what is happening in the city. Movies, plays, and concerts are listed with the time, place, and sometimes the ticket prices for each performance. Special happenings are also fully described, such as fairs, festivals, parades, and such exciting events as the Auto Show and the Boat Show. There are stories or reviews of many of the happenings to help you choose things that you will enjoy.

Bring a newspaper to class. Look at the Entertainment Section. Choose something that you would like to do this weekend. On a separate sheet of paper, answer the following questions about it.

1. What is it?
2. Where is it?
3. What time is it?
4. How much will it cost?

HELP COLUMNS

ACTION COLUMNS

Most newspapers have an action column to help people solve problems and to answer questions. People often write or call this column when they have a problem which they cannot solve. The action columns help people who buy things and are unhappy or dissatisfied with the product. People who buy things are called consumers.

There are special employees on the newspaper staff to work on solving problems and finding answers to questions. Sometimes the newspapers will print problems similar to ones you have. Reading this column can help you with your daily life.

ADVICE COLUMNS

There are also columns to help those who have various personal problems. These are called advice columns. Ann Landers and Dear Abby are famous for their advice. Sometimes, a newspaper has its own advice columnist. People of all ages write for help with their personal problems. Reading this column can help you with your own problems and can often make you feel lucky that your life is not so bad!

Think about a problem you have or imagine one. On a separate sheet of paper, write a letter to your favorite advice columnist for help.

COMICS

Comics are a favorite for many. They rush to see what will go wrong next for Charlie Brown, how Archie is doing with his girlfriends, Betty and Veronica, or what trouble Beetle Baily has gotten into now. Comics are fun to read.

FOOD

One day each week, newspapers generally print a Food Section. If you enjoy food, like to cook, or do the grocery shopping, the Food Section is often fun and helpful to read. It has recipes for many different kinds of food and articles which will help you plan healthy meals. It also contains stories that teach people new skills, such as how to store or preserve foods.

Grocery shoppers read this section to find the best values in order to save money. Many stores have large ads in this section that list grocery items which are on sale. Readers compare prices to choose the best place to shop. Sometimes, there are coupons which will refund you money if you buy certain products. Smart shoppers read the Food Section.

EDITORIALS

The Editorial Page is where the editors of a newspaper write about their own feelings and opinions. They discuss happenings, events and problems in the community. The activities of the government in cities, states, and in our national capital in Washington, D.C. are often the subject of editorials. Newspapers try to discuss topics of concern to their readers and try to explain the news of the day by giving more information and facts. The Editorial Page is the only part of the paper where opinions are given.

Editorials help people to think and to form opinions. This often occurs when elections are held. Editorials give information about the people who are running for office, who are called candidates. Newspapers talk about the candidates' qualifications and abilities, and they suggest those whom we should vote for.

Most newspapers also include letters from their readers on the editorial page. People often want to express their own feelings about happenings in their community. Their letters will show many different emotions, from anger to praise.

TELEVISION/RADIO

Radio and television programs are listed each day in the newspaper. As a service to its readers, a newspaper lists the time and station for programs, to help readers choose what they want to hear and see.

Look at the television listings. Discuss these questions with your classmates.

1. What program is on channel 2 at 7:00 p.m.?
2. What movie begins at 8:00 on channel 5?
3. What channels have local news at 10:00 p.m.?
4. What football teams play at 8:00 p.m. on channel 7?
5. Channel 11, the national educational television station in Chicago, has a special program at 8:00 p.m. What is it?
6. What are your favorite television programs?

7:00 Rhoda 2
Rhoda finally gets a chance to meet Joe's ex-wife, but as the time draws near, she isn't so sure she wants to meet her after all.

Invisible Man 5
When priceless paintings are stolen from the Capitol building in Washington, D.C., Westin must find who the culprits are. Stars: David McCallum, Melinda Fee, Craig Stevens.

Barbary Coast 7
Cable and Cash are involved with a devious beauty, a ruthless art collector and a sword duel in their attempt to unite a matching set of priceless jeweled cats stolen from the Chinese government.

b Movie 9
"Golden Eye." See index.

7:30 Phyllis 2
When Phyllis' daughter goes on an overnight skiing outing, Phyllis begins to worry that the young man she's with will "try something."

World Press 11

8:00 All in the Family . 2
Mike declares his and Gloria's moving day as "independence day," and verbal fireworks begin.

Movie 5
"April Fools." See index.

Football 7
Dallas Cowboys vs. N.Y. Jets, in Dallas.

Vienna Symphony Orchestra 11
See Highlights.

Sammy and Company 9
Guests: Sandy Duncan, Roger Miller, Aaron Spelling, Karen Valentine.

8:30 Maude 2
When Maude decides to run for the state senate, Walter decides to run for the nearest swinging-singles bachelor pad.

9:00 Medical Center ... 2
See Highlights.

Compositores de Mexico 26

Mary Jane Odell and Other Voices ... 26
See Highlights.

9:30 Report from Mexico City 11
Shana Alexander reports on the International Women's Year Conference.

10:00 Local News .. 2,5,9

Jean Shepherd's America 11
Rerun. Shepherd witnesses what happens when four Midwesterners try deep-sea fishing off the coast of Florida.

PROFESSIONAL HOCKEY
HIGH SCHOOL GYMNASTICS

SPORTS

Many people enjoy following sports. Fans often turn to this section of the paper first, to see if their favorite team won the game. High school, college, and professional sports are all reported. Scores of games, exciting photographs, and stories about games and players make interesting reading for sports fans.

There are major sports each season—football in the fall, basketball in the winter, baseball in the spring and summer. But, many other sports are growing in popularity. These include tennis, hockey, golf, horse racing, skiing, swimming, track, wrestling, gymnastics, soccer, and many, many more. The Sports Section has stories about all sports. They want all sports fans to buy the newspaper.

CLASSIFIED ADVERTISING

Newspapers have a special section for classified ads. These advertisements are classified or organized into special categories. This helps readers to find what they are looking for and helps the people of a community to buy, sell, trade, and do business together. These advertisements are often called "Want Ads". People use these ads to find many things they need. Are you looking for a job? Do you need a place to live? Do you want to sell your motorcycle? Are you looking for a used car to buy? Did you lose your dog? Classified ads can help people find all these answers and many more.

THE CLASSIFIED INDEX

There is a special index for the classified ads so that they are easy to use. All the ads are also listed in alphabetical order.

Look at the sample index. *Air Conditioning, Apartments to Rent,* and *Automobiles* are listed under the letter A. *Cameras and Optical Equipment* and *Counseling Service* are in the listings beginning with the letter C. The F listings include *Florists* and *Furniture and Furnishings.*

index

Use the index to the classified ads. On a separate sheet of paper, write the page number where you can find ads about each of the following.

1. You are looking for a job. Check the Help Wanted ads.
2. You lost your wallet. Look under Lost and Found.
3. You want to buy a TV set. Look under Television.
4. You need to find a place to live. Check the Apartments to Rent.
5. You want to buy something special and there is no listing for it. You might find it under Miscellaneous (For Sale).

People and businesses place ads in the classified section. They know readers will look there when they want something. People who want to sell things, people who want to advertise their services, and businesses who want to hire people use the want ads.

All these ads cost money. The advertising space is sold per line and per day. Thus, an ad of *four lines* which will appear in a newspaper for *five days* might cost $8.00. Since people must pay for each line, they try to word their ad to say what they want in the shortest space possible. They often use abbreviations to save space and say as much as possible in fewer lines.

HELP WANTED ADS

Help Wanted Ads are placed by businesses when they want to hire people. People who are job hunting check the Help Wanted Ads to find jobs which sound interesting to them and which match their skills. The ads usually list either a phone number or an address of the person who should be contacted. When you find a job that you would like, you may need to fill out an employment application (which you know how to do) and go see the possible employer for an interview. There will usually be lots of people interested in the same job.

Help Wanted Ads use many abbreviations. Being able to read the abbreviations makes using the want ads easy.

Look at these sample Help Wanted Ads and the abbreviations used in them. There are, of course, many other abbreviations that are used.

Ad	Abbreviations
GENERAL OFFICE-Insurance office needs alert person for **sec.** & **misc.** office responsibilities. Must be accurate and enjoy detail. **Exc.** benefits and **sal. N. Sub.** 1 **blk.** from **pub. trans.** 172-5107	secretary miscellaneous excellent salary North suburb 1 block from public transportation
BEAUTICIAN-FULL TIME. Some **exp. nec. Gd.** pay and **pd.** vacation. 102-0824. **Aft. 8 P.M.** 104-7102.	experience necessary good paid after 8 at night
COOK-w/training and 2 **yrs. rest. exp.** No **Sun.** or **holi.** Day **hrs.** Apply in person. 405 E. Jefferson Street 8 A.M. to 3 P.M.	years restaurant, experienced Sunday or holiday hours
CLEANING-**Exp. Gen. hswrk. Perm. Mon., Thurs., $70/wk.** 113-4519	general housework permanent Monday, Thursday $70 dollars per week

Bring the classified ads section of a newspaper to class. Under the Help Wanted Ads, find a job which sounds good to you. Can you find the answers to these questions in the ad you selected? Write or discuss your answers on a separate sheet of paper.

1. What kind of work is the job?
2. Do you need experience for the job?
3. Do you have to use your own car or have a driver's license?
4. What is the salary?
5. How many days a week will you work?
6. What time would you work?
7. What telephone number should you call to apply for the job?
8. Is the address of the business given?

Discuss using the Help Wanted Ads with your classmates. What things should you look for when you are job hunting?

FOR SALE ADS

People place ads in this section when they want to sell items that they no longer need or want. There are lots of different items for sale here—furniture, clothes, cameras, cars, stereos, books, and fishing equipment. There is usually a phone number to call if you are interested. The price is often listed, too. When a person wants to buy something, the classified ads are a good place to look.

Look at these For Sale Ads. There are many abbreviations used in the ads. Some abbreviations are explained below.

Ad	Abbreviations
PANASONIC-Stereo, 4 **wks.** old. A.M.-F.M. $110-best **ofr.** Hitachi **B&W** TV 19″ solid state, 4 **wks.** old-$100-best offer. 642-4387	weeks offer black and white
DIN RM SET-6 **capt. chrs., tbl.,** server., break front, pecan wood, like new $650. **Mon. thru Sat. betw.** 9&11 am 955-3745	dining room set captain chairs, table Monday thru Saturday between
BUICK-'70 Electra 225 **4dr. hdtp.** Clean-1 owner, full power, **A/C,** radials $1590. 676-4777 or 965-0078 **eves.**	four door, hardtop air conditioning evenings

Read the For Sale Ads and use the keys for the abbreviations. Figure out the answers to the following questions.

1. Which item costs the most?
2. How old is the stereo that is for sale?
3. How much would the stove and refrigerator cost all together?
4. What year is the Buick which is for sale? What model?

SITUATIONS WANTED

People who are looking for a certain job might want to advertise their skills. In Situation Wanted Ads, you must mention what kind of work you want, your experience, and how you can be contacted.

Look at these Situation Wanted Ads. Many abbreviations in these ads are used to save space and money. The abbreviations used in these sample ads are explained below.

PAINTER-experienced. Interior & exterior. **Reas.** rates. Materials **incl.** Free **est.** 487-7049	reasonable rates included free estimate
CLEANING-**Exp.** woman **w/refs.** seeking day work. 387-7218	experienced with references
L.P.N.-Good reference. With car. Will live in. 955-8202	Licensed Practical Nurse
CARPENTER-Old timer. Specialty on porches. 50 **yrs. exp. Reas.** Free estimate. 545-6257	50 years of experience reasonable (price)

Now use the Situation Wanted Ads and the abbreviation key to answer the following questions.

1. In the PAINTER's ad, what does "interior & exterior" mean?
2. What does "with references" mean in the ad for CLEANING?
3. In the ad for an L.P.N., what does "will live in" mean?
4. What is the meaning of "free estimate" in the ad for a CARPENTER?

LOST AND FOUND

Ads are placed in this section when someone has lost something of value. Sometimes, money is offered as a reward if the lost items are returned. When people find things, they read these ads so they can return what they found to the owner. Sometimes, a person who finds something will place an ad under the heading FOUND.

These ads were placed by people who have lost or found something. Many abbreviations are used which are explained below. Read the ads and answer or discuss the questions about them which follow.

BRIEFCASE-Lost, **Vic.**-63rd & Halsted. **Blk. Apprec.** if returned **w/**contract papers. $25 **Rew.** 731-5118	vicinity (near) black appreciate with $25 reward
WATCH LOST-4/20/75. **Museum of Sci. & Ind. Rew.** 371-8982	Museum of Science and Industry reward
DOG FOUND-9/7. **Nr.** Kennedy **Xwy.** + North **Ave.** Male, about 3 **mos. Blk. and tan.** Day-489-5900, **Eve.**-835-1131	near expressway avenue 3 months old black and tan evenings

1. What is the reward for the return of the BRIEFCASE?
2. When was the WATCH lost?
3. How old is the found DOG?

FOR RENT

People often need to find a place to live. Many people rent apartments and houses. The For Rent section of the classified ads will help anyone find housing. Apartments for rent are listed separately from houses for rent. There are also separate listings for those which are furnished and those that are unfurnished.

When looking for a place to live, one is concerned about the location, size, price, and furnishings or appliances. The ads should answer these questions and help the readers decide which ads they should call about.

Read these For Rent ads and look at the abbreviations. Then, answer the questions which follow.

Ad	Abbreviations
STREAMWOOD-LIKE NEW 3 **lg.** bedrooms, huge living **rm.**, super kitchen, full carpeting, drapes. Trees, **gar.** $285 884-1111	large room garage
3 **bdrms., furn. bsmt. apt., kit.** & bath. Roseland. $135+**sec.** 468-7066 **aft.** 4 pm	bedrooms, furnished basement apartment kitchen, security deposit after
STUDIO **apt.**, in **vic.** DEVON & HARLEM, **avail.** now, $190. **Ht., stv., refrg., air cond.,** cooking gas. **Ful. crpt.** 299-7855	vicinity available heat, stove, refrigerator air conditioning fully carpeted

1. What does "full carpeting and drapes" mean in the ad for the house in Streamwood?
2. How many bedrooms are there in the house in Skokie?
3. What is the meaning of $135 + sec. in the ad for the 3 room apartment?
4. What things are included in the studio apartment?

THE WEATHER REPORT

The weather report is in the newspaper every day. It helps in planning what kind of clothing you should wear and if you will need a raincoat, umbrella or boots. A long trip might need to be delayed if a bad snowstorm is coming. A frost warning tells people that they must cover up their plants. The weather report also has a map to show the weather in other parts of the country. This map will show where there are storms and give the temperatures in different parts of the country.

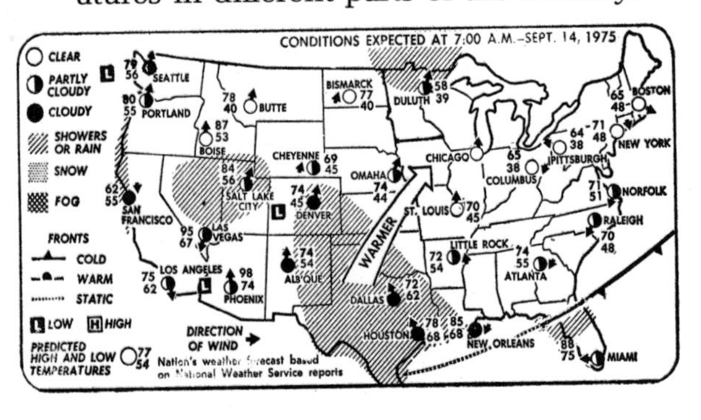

DEATHS/OBITUARIES

The obituaries are a daily listing of all the people who have died. It also tells the members of the family and friends the time and place of the funeral service and the place of burial. Sometimes newspapers will write a short article about the life of a person who was well known.

FACT/OPINION

There is a big difference between fact and opinion. It is an important difference to understand.

Facts are true statements which can be proven. Most newspaper reports are facts. "The United States is a country", is a fact.

Opinions are personal feelings. Many people might feel the same way about something, but that still doesn't make it a fact. For example, many Americans think that, "The United States is the best country of all." However, it is still not a fact. Newspapers should only express their opinions and feelings on the editorial page.

Can you tell the difference between a fact and an opinion? Sometimes, it is not easy to tell the difference, especially when an opinion is popular and believed by many people.

Look at the following statements. On a separate sheet of paper, number from 1 to 10. Write *fact,* if the statement is true. Write *opinion* if it states a personal feeling.

1. Mr. Adams was mayor of the city from 1975 to 1979.
2. Mr. Adams is a very nice man.
3. Plants will die if they do not get any water.
4. Tulips are the prettiest flowers of all.
5. Milk is important for strong bones and teeth.
6. Everyone likes milk.
7. Small cars look better than big ones.
8. The Ford Motor Company makes automobiles.
9. San Francisco is a city in California.
10. San Francisco is the best city in the world.

Chapter FOURTEEN

AM I ABLE TO USE MY LANGUAGE IN PRACTICAL WAYS?

ADVERTISING TECHNIQUES

Every minute of every day, we are targets for advertisements. Advertisers bombard us with words and pictures in magazines and newspapers, and on billboards and television. The radio is filled with advertising messages, too. Advertisers want us to buy certain things, eat certain foods, and go to certain places. Through advertising, we also learn about new products.

Advertising is expensive. People must buy the product to make advertising pay. An ad on TV or in a magazine will cost several thousand dollars. But, hopefully, millions of people will see the ad, and thousands of them will buy the product. Remember that a part of a product's price goes to pay for the advertising.

Ads make people want to buy a certain toothpaste that does a better job of fighting germs, a certain soap that will make us clean and beautiful, a certain mouthwash so we'll have lots of friends, etc.

There are three goals of advertising:

1. to attract our attention
2. to introduce new products and ideas
3. to make us form certain opinions

In this ad, the illustration attracts your attention. Then, you read and learn about the product. The advertisers want you to form a good opinion about the product. After you see an ad, they want you to think, "I'd like to try that." Then, they hope you'll go out and buy it.

People who buy things are called consumers. Advertisers try to get consumers to buy certain things. They use many different methods to sell their products. Some of these methods are:

Testimonial

A famous or well known person promotes a certain product. The advertisers hope that consumers will try the product just because a special person uses it.

Plain Folks

People in everyday situations use a certain product. Sometimes, an advertisement is set up like a testimonial, only now the product is used by people just like us, instead of a famous person. We can see ourselves in the same situations. We see ourselves needing the product, and we buy it.

Bandwagon

The ad says that everybody is buying the product. We want to try something that everyone else is using, so we buy the product.

Card Stacking

An ad gives information about a product. However, only certain facts are given, while other information is left out. The product will often be compared to a competitor. But, the comparison will be incomplete. People want to buy the product, because, from the facts given, the product seems good.

Transfer

An ad shows a very special idea, feeling, or situation. The advertiser wants people to think that they'll get that same special feeling or be in the special situation if they buy the product.

Advertisers use the above techniques to make people want certain products. These following sample advertisements actually show how the above methods are used. Look at what each ad is trying to do and how it is trying to sell the product. Think about the questions for each example, too.

TESTIMONIAL

1. Do you know whether or not the person really uses the product?
2. Do you think some famous people might do an ad just for the money or for the publicity and not really use the product?
3. Do you think famous people are experts on all things?
4. Does a famous person in a "testimonial" ad make you want to try a product?

PLAIN FOLKS

1. Is this a real person doing real life things, or is this person a model?
2. Why would an ad use a typical person to sell a product?
3. Does seeing "real people" in an ad make you want to try a product?

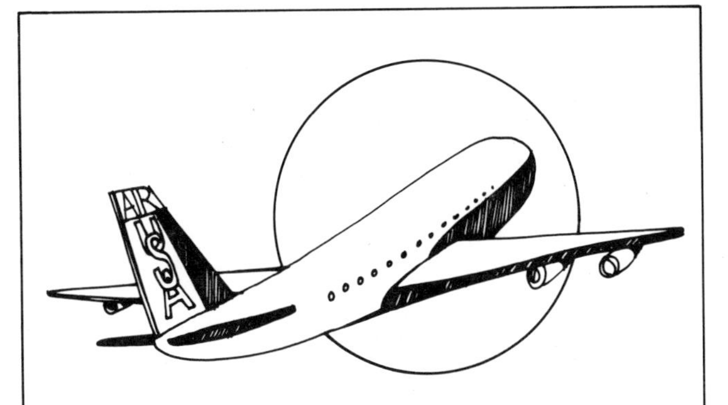

THIS IS AMERICA'S FAVORITE AIRLINE

AIR U.S.A. is America's No. 1 airline. Most people prefer our spacious lounge, wide aisles and seats, enjoy our films, music and games and take advantage of our convenient reservation system. SO DON'T SETTLE FOR LESS!

IT'S AMERICA'S FAVORITE

BANDWAGON

1. Do you know if the airline is really America's favorite? (Read this ad. They assume that all other airlines offer less.)
2. Why would the ad try to say that most people prefer this airline?
3. Do you want to use an airline when you think that most everyone else uses it?

CARD STACKING

1. What information is given about the product that makes people want to buy it?
2. Are there any facts left out?
3. Do you think most people look carefully at ads like this? Do you think people realize that some facts are left out?

TRANSFER

1. Does the product have anything to do with the person?
2. Will the same thing happen to any girl who buys the product?
3. Do you learn anything about a product from this kind of advertising?

On a separate sheet of paper, write the method used in each of these examples of advertising. Choose from testimonial, real people, bandwagon, card stacking, and transfer.

1. A girl is shown in three different pictures—studying, playing tennis, and on a date with her boyfriend. She says that there is only one perfume that is right for her and her kind of life, and her life is really just like yours.
2. An ad shows a person suffering from a cold. A man appears and says that 3 out of 4 people suffering from colds use a certain capsule which gives them 12 hours of relief from their cold symptoms. 75% of all cold sufferers use this certain cold remedy because it works.
3. A man and woman are running along a beautiful beach. It is evening. They are in love. The woman uses a certain brand of hair color.
4. A famous tennis player is pictured holding her tennis racket. She talks about how she spends many hours in the sun every day. She says that she always uses a certain suntan lotion.
5. An ad shows a roll of paper towels. It says that this brand of paper towels is stronger than any other brand.

FOLLOWING DIRECTIONS

People need to follow directions every day—in school, in their jobs, and at home. Reading directions to find out how to do something is a part of everyday living. An example is when you make a phone call. You must follow directions to dial the number you want. If you are not careful, you may lose your money in a pay phone, get a wrong number, or just waste a lot of time.

Many people enjoy making things. They must follow directions to build a book shelf, knit a scarf, or bake chocolate chip cookies. Many things that you buy must be put together at home, by following directions.

Directions are very important when you buy something new. Imagine that you just got a new alarm clock. You would need to read the directions very carefully so you could set it for the correct time. You would also need to follow the directions to turn off the alarm. In a few days, using the alarm clock generally becomes a habit. But, when you first get something new, reading the directions is very important.

People must follow directions in their jobs, so that they do not make mistakes. Learning to follow directions is an important skill.

You must read and listen to directions in school every day. Following classroom directions can help you learn to listen and to think carefully.

Read the directions for the two exercises on this and the following page. Do your work on a separate sheet of paper. See how well you can follow directions.

In this exercise, the name of a group of things is given first. After the group name, five words are listed. One of the words does not belong with the group. Which word is it? On a separate sheet of paper, number from 1 to 10. Write the word that does not belong in each group.

1. FRUIT apple, book, pear, peach, grape
2. SCHOOL notebook, pencils, teachers, desks, airplane
3. NEWSPAPER printing, articles, ads, dirt, index
4. CAR wheels, hood, doors, trunk, silk
5. PICNIC curtains, ants, napkins, food, pop
6. ANIMALS dog, zebra, elephant, tiger, paper
7. SPORTS tennis, hockey, bubblegum, baseball, basketball
8. COLORS red, blue, green, wood, brown
9. FISH perch, bee, bass, goldfish, trout
10. STATES Ohio, Nevada, Nashville, Texas, Maine

Number your paper from 1 to 10. If a statement is true, write T. If a statement is false, write F. Rewrite each false statement to make it true.

1. Words are listed alphabetically in a dictionary.
2. There are three guide words on each page.
3. All words have only one meaning.
4. A pronunciation key helps us pronounce letters.
5. An illustration is a picture.
6. There are two columns of words on each page of all dictionaries.
7. The guide word at the top of the left hand column is the first word defined on that page.
8. Sometimes, a dictionary gives sentences which show how to use a word.
9. There are no words that begin with the letter "Z" in a dictionary.
10. Words are divided into syllables in a dictionary.

GIVING DIRECTIONS

People often need to find out how to get from one place to another. You might need to give a friend the directions to your home. Sometime, a stranger may stop and ask you for directions to a certain place. You need to be careful and accurate when you give directions so that people do not get lost.

The words *north, south, east,* and *west* name directions. The words *right* and *left* are useful, too. Landmarks, objects, and places along the way, such as a gas station, stoplight, or restaurant, can make directions easier to follow.

Let's imagine a time you might have to give directions. Suppose a new boy moves into your apartment building. You walk to school everyday, but you have to leave early for swimming practice. You give him these directions.

> Face the street in front of the building. Turn right and walk to the corner. Turn left, cross the street, and walk about two blocks to the corner of Grand Avenue and Market Street. There is a mailbox on the corner. Turn right and walk until you get to the park, which is about four blocks. Turn left and walk a half block to the school.

On a separate sheet of paper, write the directions for walking from your school to your home. In your directions, use the words right and left, street names, and special places and things along the way.

Often, people need to stop and ask for directions when they are in a strange or new place. If someone asks you for directions, be sure you know the way. Give the directions very carefully, because the person probably doesn't know the area. If you don't know the way, just say that you are sorry but you can't give the directions. Giving the wrong directions is unkind, unfair, and could be very serious.

Pretend there is a new student in your English class who needs to go to the main office after class. On a separate sheet of paper, write the directions to get to the main office from your English classroom.

CONFUSING WORDS

There are many words in our language which look and sound very much alike. Sometimes when we hear or read these words, it is difficult to tell them apart. Look at the following pairs of confusing words. Study each group and learn to use them correctly.

Group I

then—tells the time that something happens
than—used when comparing people or things

course—a school subject
chorus—a singing group

quite—a big amount, very
quiet—no noise

On a separate sheet of paper, number from 1 to 6. Write the correct word for each sentence.

1. Some people say that no place is more beautiful (then, than) Paris, France in the springtime.
2. If you go there in spring, (then, than) you will see all the flowers in bloom.
3. Most American high schools teach a (course, chorus) in French.
4. Our (course, chorus) sang some French songs in their last concert.
5. After touring the busy streets of Paris, people enjoy the (quiet, quite) of the famous church, Notre Dame.
6. With twelve streets surrounding the Arc de Triomphe, there is (quiet, quite) a bit of traffic.

ARC DE TRIOMPHE

Group II

purpose—reason
propose—suggest; ask to marry

loose—not tight, free
lose—not to have anymore, not be able to find something

dessert—food eaten after dinner which is usually sweet
desert—large sandy area

On a separate sheet of paper, number from 1 to 6. Write the correct word for each sentence.

1. Some men (purpose, propose) marriage to their girlfriends along the edge of the famous Seine River in Paris.
2. Some people travel to far away places such as Paris for the (purpose, propose) of learning how other people live.
3. A dog got (loose, lose) and ran through the park.
4. Paris never seems to (loose, lose) its beauty and charm.
5. One artist painted a picture of camels in a (desert, dessert).
6. Many Parisians like to eat fruit for (desert, dessert).

Group III

sweet—having the flavor of sugar
sweat—water coming from the body when it is hot

cloths—pieces or scraps of material
clothes—items worn on the body

science—a special subject studied in school
since—because

Number your paper from 1 to 6, and write the correct word for each sentence.

1. Special (sweet, sweat) baked goods, such as rolls and cakes, are sold in little stores in Paris.
2. Walking around in the hot sunlight causes many tourists to (sweet, sweat).
3. Parisians wear (clothes, cloths) much like Americans wear.
4. Wet (clothes, cloths) are used to wipe off the tables in the outdoor cafes.
5. Some students studied their (science, since) books on the grass in front of the church.
6. (Science, Since) the city is so beautiful, many people like to be outdoors.

Group IV

accept—to receive
except—but, leave something out

receipt—paper given as proof that something was purchased
recipe—directions to follow when cooking

affect—causing a change
effect—result

Number your paper from 1 to 6, and write the correct word for each sentence.

1. Everybody, (accept, except) those people who are afraid of high places, enjoy climbing the Eiffel Tower.
2. Diners in Parisian restaurants (accept, except) their checks from waiters called garçons.
3. At the airport, tourists must show the customs' agent the (receipt, recipe) for each item that they bought.
4. A French cook might give you a (receipt, recipe) to try when you get home.
5. Hearing a different language and using a different kind of money can (affect, effect) the way a visitor acts.
6. What (affect, effect) do you think these things would have on you?

EIFFEL TOWER

Group V

slept—past tense of sleep
slipped—past tense of slip (fall)

except—something left out
expect—wait for

mouth—the opening on your face that is used when eating, talking, breathing, etc.
month—one of the twelve parts of the year

On a separate sheet of paper, number from 1 to 6. Write the correct word for each sentence.

1. Many people said they hadn't (slept, slipped) much during their visit to Paris.
2. My friend (slept, slipped) on some ice at the airport when he returned to the U.S.
3. Many tourists said they had seen everything they wanted to see in Paris, (except, expect) the Opera.
4. Many people (except, expect) to visit Paris sometime during their lives.
5. A (mouth, month) in Paris will seem very short.
6. The way a person's (mouth, month) turns into a smile after returning from Paris, says it was a good place to visit.

MEETINGS

Meetings are when the members of clubs or organizations get together. Then, they take care of their club's business. Have you attended a meeting of the pep club, the student council, or another club at your school? What other kinds of clubs and meetings are there in your school and your community?

When a group of people get together, they often follow a set of rules to keep the meeting orderly. Then, they can complete their business and save time. Nothing gets done if everyone talks at once.

Agenda

I Call to Order

II Reports

A Secretary's minutes

B Treasurer's Report

C Committee Report

III Old Business

IV New Business

V Adjournment

Meetings usually follow an agenda. An agenda is an outline of what happens at a meeting.

Most meetings are run by the club's president. The president must see that parliamentary rules are followed and that the meeting goes smoothly. A meeting begins when the president says, "The meeting will now come to order," and hits a gavel on the table. The noise of the gavel hitting always tells people to be quiet.

Then, the president asks, "Will the secretary please read the minutes of the last meeting?" Minutes are a report of everything that happened at a meeting. The secretary takes notes during the meeting and records what people discuss and the votes which are taken. The minutes are always read at the next meeting.

Next, the president says, "May we have the treasurer's report?" The treasurer of a club keeps a record of all the money collected and spent. The treasurer's report tells all the transactions made since the last meeting.

Then, the president asks, "Are there any reports from committees?" Sometimes, a small group of club members work together on a special project. These small groups are called committees. They report what they are doing to everyone at the meeting.

Now, the meeting takes care of its *old business. Old business* is any topic which was talked about at a meeting in the past. When the president asks, "Is there any old business?", members can bring up things which were left unfinished at the last meeting. But no member can speak until the president gives permission. Then, they can talk without being interrupted.

When all the old business has been discussed, the president may say, "Is there any *new business*?" All new ideas and projects are *new business,* and club members can discuss them now.

There will be many things that the club members must decide. Then, a vote must be taken.

Let's imagine that a club wanted to decide when to hold their spring dance. Someone might stand and say, "I move that the dance be held on Saturday, April 21." Then, someone who agrees will say, "I second the motion." After the members have discussed holding their dance on April 21, the president calls for a voice vote, saying, "All those in favor say, 'aye' and those opposed say, 'no'." If most people say "aye", the president will say, "The motion is carried." The dance will be held on April 21. If most members say "no", a different date will have to be set.

If the vote is very close, it might be necessary to vote again. This time the president might ask people to raise their hands, instead of saying aye or no.

When it is late or all the business is completed, someone may stand and say, "I move that the meeting be adjourned." Adjourned means ended until another time.

Then, someone must second the motion.

The president says, "It has been moved and seconded that the meeting be adjourned. All those in favor say, 'aye'. All those opposed say, 'no'." If most of the members say "aye", the president will say, "This meeting is adjourned."

Meetings can be lots of fun. Everyone's ideas and suggestions are important. Never be afraid to say what you are thinking at a meeting. Share your ideas!

On a separate sheet of paper, answer the following questions.

1. Why are rules necessary at a meeting?
2. Who calls the meeting to order?
3. What are the duties of the secretary?
4. What is the job of the treasurer?
5. What is a committee?
6. What is old business?

7. Who gives members permission to speak at a meeting?
8. What does adjourn mean?
9. How are votes taken at a meeting?
10. What does it mean when the president says, "The motion is carried."?

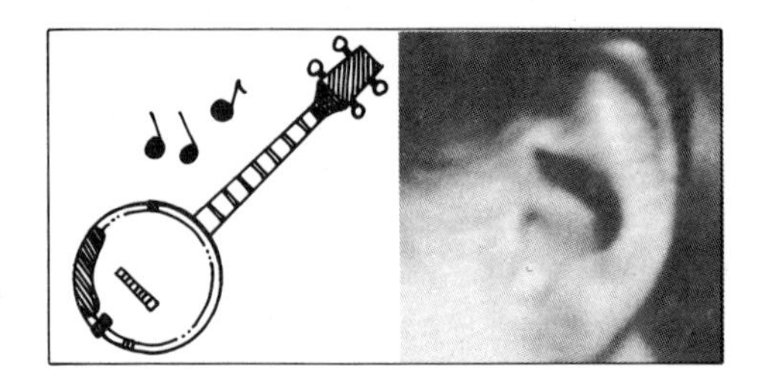

Chapter FIFTEEN

WHAT ARE MY SENSES?

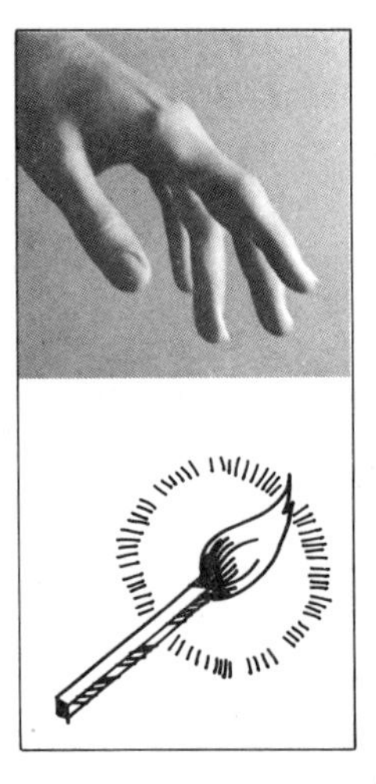

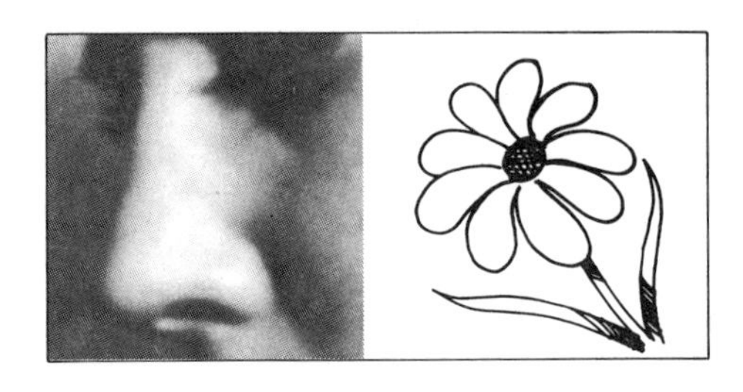

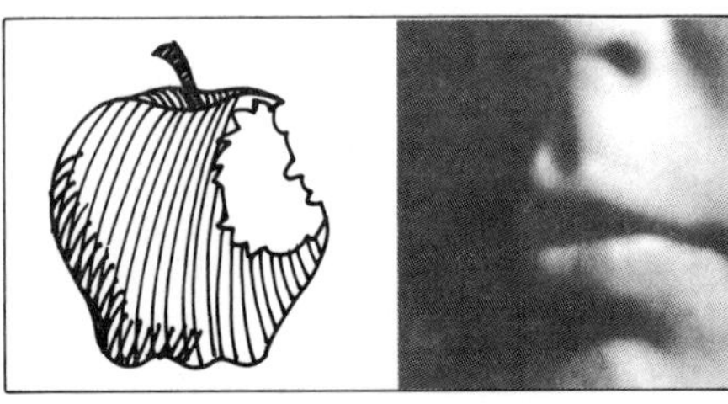

PHYSICAL SENSES

What are the five senses? Senses are special abilities in the bodies of people and animals. Our five senses of **sight, smell, taste, touch,** and **hearing** receive information from the world around us. Messages from each sense go to special areas of the brain. After the brain receives the message, the body reacts. When people see a speeding car, they try to get out of the way. When people smell good food cooking, they get hungry and want to eat. If something tastes too sour, a person will make a face. Touching a hot dish from the oven makes people pull their hands away very quickly. Hearing beautiful music makes some people very happy.

SIGHT

Let's think about the sense of sight. Seeing lets us appreciate the golden sunset on a hot summer night. Seeing lets us enjoy the first sparkling snowfall of winter. Sometimes, people see things so often that they forget to notice details. Without looking right now, do you know the color of your teacher's eyes? What color is the bottom stripe of the American flag? Could you draw a picture of a cat so that someone else could tell that it's a cat?

Take time to notice and appreciate the things you see around you everyday. The sense of sight lets people discover and enjoy many things.

On a separate sheet of paper, answer the following questions. If you don't know the answers now, look carefully after school. Be ready to discuss your answers in class tomorrow.

1. Whose picture is on the one dollar bill?
2. What color is your kitchen at home?
3. Describe your dishes at home.
4. What color are your best friend's eyes?
5. What kind and color car does your next door neighbor drive?

SMELL

The sense of smell helps us to enjoy our favorite foods. It can also warn us of danger, for example, something burning. Many animals depend on the sense of smell more than their other senses. Think about how dogs act when they are given something new. What do dogs do when they meet a new person? How else can dogs use their sense of smell?

Your teacher will read you a list of things which have very unique odors. Close your eyes. Try to imagine how each thing really smells. Try to describe each aroma.

1. the smell of grass right after it has been cut
2. a pile of dry leaves on a warm fall afternoon
3. a can of paint with the lid off
4. a freshly mimeographed sheet from your English teacher
5. a pot of freshly brewed coffee
6. a rose
7. the chlorine and chemicals in a swimming pool
8. the gym after lots of people have been sweating
9. peanut butter
10. gasoline being pumped into your car

TASTE

When we eat and drink, messages are sent from the tongue to the brain. This is our sense of taste. Actually, we depend on our sense of smell for our sense of taste to work. Before we taste, our noses send messages of smell to our brains. These messages help us react to the taste.

Try this experiment. Cut a small piece of peeled apple and a small piece of peeled onion. Cover your eyes with a cloth or blindfold. Hold your nose tightly so you cannot smell. Now, take and chew both pieces. Can you tell which is which? Most people can't tell the difference using only their sense of taste. They need their sense of smell, too.

People have four different kinds of taste. They are **sweet, salty, sour,** and **bitter**. Different areas on your tongue react to different tastes, and send the messages to your brain.

On a separate sheet of paper, make a list of your five favorite foods and the five foods you dislike the most. After each food, write which kind of taste it has, either sweet, salty, sour, or bitter. Think about the odor that goes with each food, too.

TOUCH

All of our skin is sensitive and sends messages to the brain. But, our hands, and especially the tips of our fingers, are most useful for the sense of touch. Through touch, we can feel the difference between hard and soft, rough and smooth, hot and cold. The sense of touch warns us that fire is hot. Touching lets us feel the coldness of snow. The top of your desk feels smooth, while the bark of a tree feels very rough. A book feels hard, while a pillow feels soft.

People who are blind can use the sense of touch to help them make up for their loss of sight. They can read by learning a new alphabet of raised dots. This method of reading is called Braille.

Bring something to class which you think feels different from most everything else. Close your eyes and touch something which one of your classmates has brought. Write a few sentences that describe what you felt. Can you identify what you touched?

Try this experiment with five different things. Then, share your sentences with your class.

HEARING

Ears give people their sense of hearing. There are so many sounds around us, that we often tune out many of them. Close your eyes and listen for one minute. What sounds did you hear? Did you hear anything that you hadn't heard before?

Your ears let you hear many sounds. But, your brain will get the messages only if you think about the sounds. Thinking about the sounds you hear is called listening.

Listening is a skill which is important and easy to learn. We must train ourselves to think about everything we hear. Then, we will be good listeners.

SPECIAL ABILITIES

People are sensitive to many things and have many special abilities. Some of these are senses, but they are different from the five senses. Some of our five senses are used to perform these special abilities. These include a sense of danger, a sense of balance, a sense of humor, a sense of rhythm, and common sense.

DANGER

A sense of danger is what makes a small animal run from a larger one. Have you ever seen a bird fly away when a cat was creeping close to it? The bird felt it was unsafe to stay where it was through its sense of danger.

Have you ever been afraid when you walked down a dark street? You were alert to the possibility of danger. Your sense of danger was working, too.

BALANCE

A sense of balance keeps people from falling down. It is especially important for people involved in sports. A person needs a good sense of balance to work out on the balance beam. In a football game, the ball carrier needs a sense of balance to avoid tackles and to keep from stumbling. Hockey players, skiers, and tight rope walkers all depend on their sense of balance.

Babies are not born with a sense of balance. They fall down many times when they are first learning to walk. They must develop the special ability which keeps them from falling.

HUMOR

Having a sense of humor makes life more fun. People who have a good sense of humor are able to laugh easily and can really enjoy things that are funny.

RHYTHM

Good dancers have a good sense of rhythm. Have you ever seen someone who has difficulty keeping time with the music? A sense of rhythm is needed to play musical instruments, too. And, without it, a marching band couldn't keep in step.

COMMON SENSE

Common sense is a person's ability to choose the right thing to do. It tells us to look before we cross a street. It keeps us from saying things that would hurt someone's feelings. Don't tell your best friend you think her new sweater is ugly. Common sense keeps us from asking embarassing questions. It helps people to be sensitive to the feelings and needs of other people.

USING OUR SENSES

Everyday living requires using all five senses. To be aware of everything around us, all our senses must work together. Then, we can really enjoy and appreciate our world. People who do not have all five senses are handicapped. Their other senses must work much harder to make up for the lost one.

Practice using your senses to get as much as possible from all you do. Be sensitive to your surroundings. Train yourself to look around, to listen carefully, and to eat slowly so you can really taste. Let your nose and fingers work for you, too.

Don't forget to develop your special abilities. They can help you enjoy living.

Chapter SIXTEEN

CAN I SPELL SOUNDS AND SOUND COMBINATIONS?

We often write to communicate with each other. It is important to spell words correctly so that others can read and understand what we have written. There are basic rules for spelling and pronunciation. These rules are called **phonics**. If you learn the basic rules of phonics, both reading and writing become much easier. This chapter will focus on the sounds of letters and letter combinations which are used most often.

VOWELS

The vowels are the letters **a, e, i, o,** and **u. W** and **y** sometimes act as vowels, too. Vowels have long and short sounds. A straight line over a letter (ā), called a macron, indicates the long vowel sound. A curved line over a letter (ă), called a breve, means it has the short vowel sound. Say the sounds of each vowel and listen to the difference between them.

The Long and Short Sounds of A

	ā as in ate	ă as in apple
at the beginning of a word	able, age April, aim	add, at, am, and
in the middle of a word	hate, base, bake, baby	flat, hat, fat, pal

Copy the following words onto a separate sheet of paper. Mark the letter *a* in each word to indicate the long or short sound. The first one is done for you.

1. făn	3. mad	5. cane	7. date
2. plate	4. hand	6. ham	8. man

The Long and Short Sounds of E

	ē as in eat	ĕ as in elephant
at the beginning of a word	equal, Edith, erupt	end, enjoy, empty, Emily
in the middle or at the end of the word	be, we, he, delay	bed, pen, peg, bell

Copy the following words onto a separate sheet of paper. Mark the letter *e* in each word to indicate the long or short vowel sound.

1. jet	3. recall	5. neon	7. evil
2. elm	4. net	7. evict	8. fed

The Long and Short Sounds of I	ī as in ice	ĭ as in hit
at the beginning of a word	iron, island, item, idea	in, it, is, inch
in the middle of a word	side, size, tiger, tight	miss, sit, pin, ship

Copy the following words onto a separate sheet of paper. Mark the letter *i* in each word to indicate the long or short sound.

1. ivy	3. fix	5. ink	7. trip
2. into	4. tire	6. time	8. title

The Long and Short Sounds of O	ō as in open	ŏ as in of
at the beginning of a word	old, over, own, ocean	on, odd, off,
in the middle or at the end of a word	gold, sold, go, globe	hot, job, spot, not

Copy the following words onto a separate sheet of paper. Mark the letter *o* in each word to indicate the long or short sound.

1. top	3. hole	5. mop	7. notice
2. row	4. knot	6. coke	8. cot

The Long and Short Sounds of U

	ū as in use	ŭ as in up
at the beginning of a word	unit, union, usual, united	under, us uncle, umbrella
in the middle of a word	cute, huge, rude, mule	cup, run gum, mud

Copy the following words onto a separate sheet of paper. Mark the letter *u* in each word to indicate the long or short sound.

1. much	3. gun	5. June	7. uniform
2. universe	4. umpire	6. nut	8. sun

VOWEL COMBINATIONS

The long and short sounds of the vowels are often made by using two vowels together to make one sound. Say and study the words in each of the groups that follow. Notice how two vowels together make one vowel sound. There are several different combinations of vowels that can make the same sound.

Vowel Sound	**Vowel Combinations**	**Examples**
ā	ei	beige, veil, eight, weight, freight, neighbor
	ai	sail, wait, aid, exclaim, paid, faint, main
	ay	tray, play, stay, may, say, pay, spray, Monday
	ea	steak, great, break
ē	ee	deep, feel, steel, see, speed, sheet, sleep
	ei	either, ceiling
	ea	speak, seat, tea, ear, mean, steal, each, east
	ie	chief, thief, belief, field, relief
ĕ	ea	health, bread, death, ready, heavy, weather
ī	ie	die, pie, tie, lie
	ei	height
ō	oe	hoe, foe, toe
	oa	boat, road, toad, soap
	ow	show, snow, low, crow

Look at the vowel combination which is underlined in each of the following words. On a separate sheet of paper, write the sound that each combination makes. Choose from **a, ē, ĕ, i,** and **o.**

1. bread	4. play	6. teach	9. tree
2. die	5. boat	7. Sunday	10. weather
3. ceiling		8. heaven	

SILENT E

Some vowel sounds change from a short sound to a long sound when an *e* is added to the end of a word. This *e* is silent. It has no sound of its own.

hop⟶hope	hat⟶hate	win⟶wine
rat⟶rate	cut⟶cute	pin⟶pine

PRONOUNCING LONG AND SHORT VOWELS

Read these sentences out loud. Be sure to say the underlined words correctly, using a long or short vowel sound. Remember that an *e* at the end of a word is silent and makes the other vowel sound long.

1. We <u>bathe</u> our bodies when we take a <u>bath</u>.
2. People <u>breathe</u> rapidly when they exercise, and often must stop to catch their <u>breath</u>.
3. When he took a <u>bite</u> of his sandwich, he also <u>bit</u> his tongue.
4. It's fun to pick <u>ripe</u> apples as long as you don't <u>rip</u> your clothes while climbing the tree.
5. It is <u>not</u> right to write a <u>note</u> to your friend during class.
6. In the <u>dim</u> light he could not find a <u>dime</u> to make a phone call.
7. The <u>mad</u> dog <u>made</u> the boys run quickly to their car.
8. Our neighbors gave <u>us</u> their car to <u>use</u> when ours was in the shop.
9. After the game, everyone stopped and <u>ate</u> <u>at</u> the drive-in.
10. My little brother bought a <u>kit</u> to make a <u>kite</u>.

WHEN Y IS USED AS A VOWEL

We have already seen **y** used in vowel combinations. When combined with a vowel the **y** is silent, and the vowel is long. For example, when it is used with the letter **a**, it makes the long **a** sound, as in **day** and **tray.** It also has vowel sounds of its own.

The letter **y** sometimes has the sound of **e** at the end of a word. Pronounce these words and listen for the long sound of **e** at the end of each word.

carry	party	penny	hurry	candy	energy
lady	daily	salary	ivy	baby	happy

The letter **y** at the end of a word can also have the sound of long **i**. Pronounce these words and listen for the long sound of **i** at the end of each word.

my	sky	cry	dry
fly	fry	shy	why

The pronunciations are from the *Random House Dictionary of the English Language*, 1969.

CONSONANTS

Some consonants have more than one sound. Look at these consonants and notice that each one can be pronounced two ways.

Consonant	Sound	Example
c	s	ice, city, race, nice, cent, center, dance
	k	cake, cold, come, cream, can, cash, camp, camera, cost, clear
g	j	gym, age, package, giant, damage, manage, danger, energy
	g	grass, girl, garden, good, grape, ground, give
s	s	some, saw, sad, soft, sand, swim, sent
	z	busy, praise, noise, those, raise, cheese, please, nose

CONSONANT DIGRAPHS

Sometimes, two consonants combine to form a new sound. These are digraphs. Instead of pronouncing the sounds of the two separate consonants, we must learn a completely different sound. Pronounce these groups of words. Listen for the new sounds made by these consonant digraphs.

wh (at the beginning of a word)

where	when	wheat	white
while	whether	what	why

ch ch can have the ch sound, as in chart, the sh sound as in Chicago, and the k as in character

(at the beginning of a word)

chief	chill	chair	child
charge	chop	chest	cheap
change	chicken	chance	choose
check	chain	cheese	chapter

(at the end of a word)

rich	beach	touch	inch
lunch	bunch	ouch	teach
search	pinch	couch	ditch

sh (at the beginning of a word)

short	shop	shirt	shake
shoe	show	shelf	share
shut	shoot	shovel	should
ship	shower	sharp	

(at the end of a word)

wash	finish	flash	selfish
rash	dish	fresh	push
punish	dash	wish	cash
mash	brush	fish	rush

th *sounded*

(at the beginning of a word)

the	there	this	that
them	they	then	those

(in the middle of a word)

father	gather	leather	weather
brother	feather	clothing	bathing

th *unsounded*

(at the beginning of a word)

thousand	thick	think	thank
thimble	thirst	through	thread
throw	thirty	thing	thief

(In the middle of a word)

arithmetic nothing

(at the end of a word)

worth	health	wealth	bath
cloth	math	both	with
earth	month	teeth	path

SILENT CONSONANTS

wr When the letter **w** comes before the letter **r,** the **w** is silent.

wrong	wrist
wreath	write
wrap	wrestle

kn When the letter **k** comes before the letter **n,** the **k** is silent.

knee	knife	knit	knock
know	knob	knew	knot

Chapter SEVENTEEN

AM I AWARE OF CURRENT VOCABULARY?

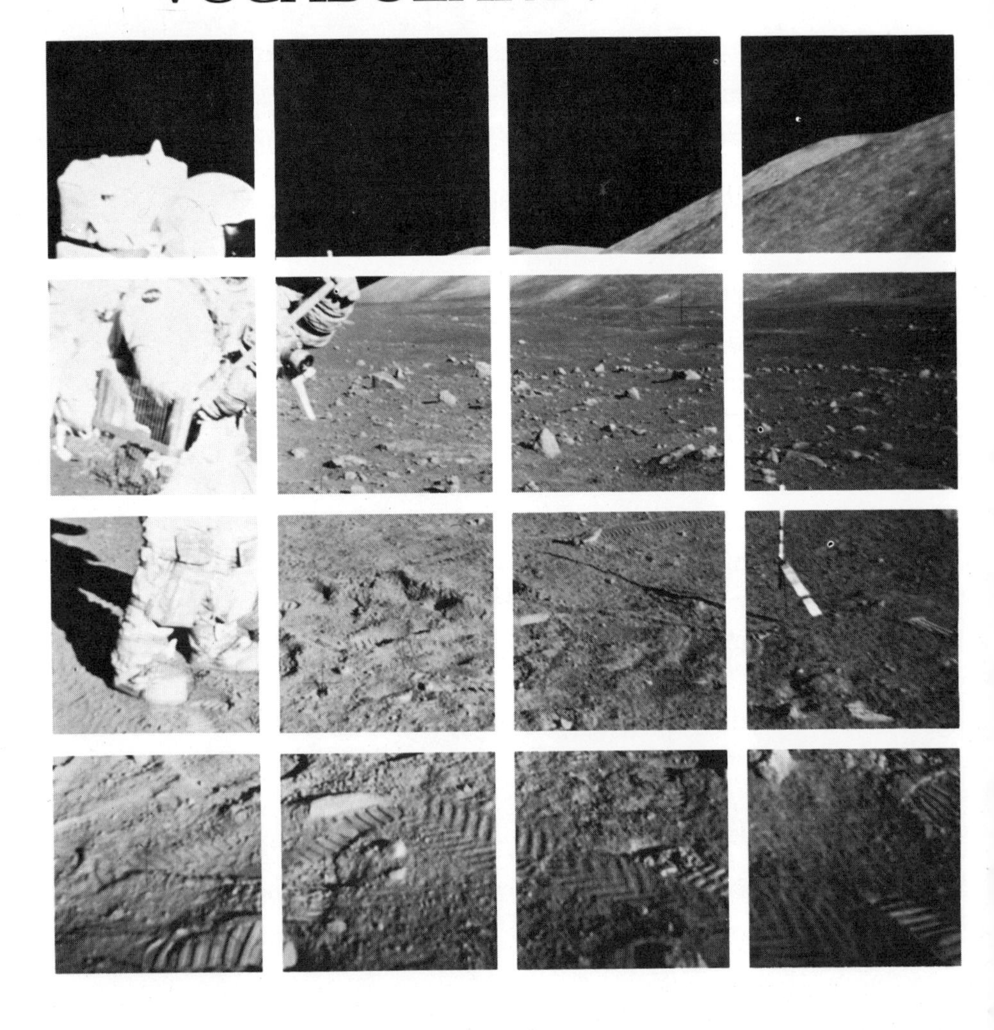

Do you ever get confused by some words that other people use? Do you ever pretend to understand, even when you aren't sure what some words mean? The English language has hundreds of thousands of words. In our everyday living, we constantly come in contact with words that we don't know. But, the more words we learn, the more we can understand in the world around us.

In this chapter, we will increase our vocabulary by learning new words. The new words are divided into groups according to different topics. First, we will learn the meanings of the new words. Then, we will practice using the words in sentences. Learning new words will help you in your everyday living.

HOME

rent	money paid to live in a place
lease	a written contract allowing the use of property, after rent is paid, for a certain time period—usually one year
occupancy	living in a place
occupant	the person who lives in a place
dwelling	a building or place to live
bungalow	a small house on one level
bi-level	a home built on two levels
tri-level	a home built on three levels
duplex	a house for two families with two separate living areas
apartment	a room or group of rooms in a larger building where people pay rent to live
condominium	an apartment which is owned by the people who live in it
furnished apartment	an apartment which already contains furniture
veranda	a porch
patio	an open cement area, usually in the back of a house.

On a separate sheet of paper, number from 1 to 14. Write the correct word from the list of **home** words for each blank.

1. A building or place where people live is a ______.
2. Joe pays his ______ money to the owner of the apartment building.
3. When a business doesn't know the name of the people living at a certain address, it sends advertisements addressed to the ______.
4. The people who live in the second floor apartment enjoy sitting on their ______.
5. If you can't afford to buy furniture, look for a ______.
6. Two new families moved into the ______, and the children played in front of the house.
7. Some people buy a ______ when they don't want all the extra work that comes with owning a house.
8. Last Sunday, her family had a barbecue on the backyard ______.
9. Susan signed a ______ for one year in her apartment.
10. After Scott found a job, he rented an ______ with his friend.
11. In Mark's ______ home, the bedrooms are on the second level.
12. When Craig and Patti got married, they bought a small ______ for their first home.
13. If anything is damaged in an apartment during your ______, you must pay for the damage.
14. In their ______ home, the family room is on the lower level, the kitchen and living room on another level, and the bedrooms are on the third level.

SHOPPING

discount	money taken off the regular price
credit	buying things now and paying for them later

charge account	a special way of buying things now and paying for them later
merchandise	things offered for sale
bargain	something that is worth more than it costs
layaway	when a store puts away something you want to buy, and you pay for it a little at a time.

On a separate sheet of paper, number from 1 to 6. Write the correct word for each blank from the list of **shopping** words.

1. The clothing store had a shipment of a new spring ______.
2. Cheryl didn't have enough money to pay for the sweater, so she put it on her ______.
3. When a person has ______, they can buy something now and pay for it later.
4. The drugstore has toothpaste at a 9¢ ______ off the regular price.
5. When Cindy bought that $50.00 dress for only $25.00, she really got a good ______.
6. Jim put the stereo on ______ at the store, so he can pay for it a little at a time.

GROCERY SHOPPING

economy size	large size at a good price
produce	fruit and vegetables
pastry	sweet baked foods
beverages	drinks
detergent	cleaning products, such as soap
preserves	fruit made into jelly or jam
dietetic	special foods made for people who want to eat less sugar
fillet	boneless piece of meat or fish

margarine — a substitute for butter made from milk and vegetable oil—also called oleo

roast — a piece of meat to be cooked in the oven

veal — meat from a baby cow (calf)

On a separate sheet of paper, number from 1 to 10. Write the correct word for each blank from the list of **grocery** words.

1. Coke, coffee, and milk are kinds of ______.
2. Apples and potatoes can be found in the ______ section of the grocery store.
3. Sometimes, it is difficult to taste the difference between butter and ______.
4. Pies, cakes, and cookies are found in the ______ section of the store.
5. Their mother bought the ______ box of laundry soap because it gave her more for her money.
6. Lupé likes to eat ______ on her toast for breakfast.
7. When Fred was trying to lose weight, he ate many ______ foods.
8. José used ______ to wash the dishes.
9. Her father bought some ______ of perch for dinner.
10. In the meat section she chose a five pound beef ______ and some ______, which is meat from a baby cow.

CLOTHING

wardrobes	closets full of clothes
mini	short for minimum—refers to a very short skirt
plaid	a colorful design with stripes crossing each other
denim	a kind of heavy cotton material
synthetics	materials made from chemicals
polyester	a material that washes easily and needs no ironing
shrinkage	material that gets smaller after washing it.

On a separate sheet of paper, number from 1 to 7. Write the correct word for each blank from the list of clothing words.

1. Blue jeans are made from a material called ______.
2. Many girls think Rhoda has one of the best ______ of anyone.
3. Many new fabrics do not have the problem of ______ when they are washed.
4. Wash and wear clothing is usually made of a material called ______.
5. The colorful ______ design is popular on shirts, slacks, and dresses.
6. Kathy likes to wear ______ skirts that show off her legs.
7. Many clothes are made of ______, which are fabrics made from chemicals.

JEWELRY

sterling	a very fine silver which is as close as possible to pure silver
gold plated	a gold layer on the outside of a metal
14 karat (kt.)	a very fine gold. Pure gold is 24 kt.
engraved	a carved design on jewelry
pendant	an object that hangs from a chain and is worn as a necklace
simulated	made to look like the real thing; a copy

solitaire	a single jewel set by itself—as in a ring
setting	the outside frame for a jewel
cameo	a raised carving set on another jewel—often of a woman's head

On a separate sheet of paper, number from 1 to 9. Write the correct word for each blank from the list of **jewelry** words.

1. For her birthday, Alice wanted a ______ on a chain to wear as a necklace.
2. The ______ jewel looked like it was real.
3. Stacy wanted only one large diamond in her ring, so she picked a ______.
4. A ______ pin has a raised carving on it.
5. Identification bracelets are ______ with a person's name on the flat part.
6. Gold comes in 10 kt., 12 kt., and ______.
7. The best silver you can buy is called ______.
8. ______ jewelry has a gold layer on the outside.
9. The part that surrounds the jewel is called the ______.

JOBS

employment	when a person gets paid for working
wages	money paid for work done
fringe benefits	extras besides wages
vacation	time off from a job
temporary	not lasting for a long time; not permanent
supervisor	a person in charge of other people
promotion	a better job given as a reward for good work
plant	a factory building and its machines
uniform	special clothing which must be worn for some jobs
apprentice	a person who is learning a skill while working at a job

assembler	a person who puts parts together
receptionist	a person whose job in an office is to talk to visitors, answer the phone, and schedule appointments
overtime	extra work hours over the regular work week
deduction	money taken out of one's wages for taxes, social security, etc.

On a separate sheet of paper, number 1 to 14. Write the correct word for each blank from the list of **job** words.

1. The _____ gave Mr. Ryan an appointment for 2:00 on Thursday afternoon.
2. It is sometimes very noisy in the _____ when all the machines are running.
3. The _____ assigns jobs to the people who work under him.
4. This company gives all its workers a paid two week _____ .
5. The workers are paid their _____ by check, not in cash.
6. An _____ has the job of putting parts together.
7. Paid insurance and sick leave are examples of _____ which are given in addition to regular pay.
8. Because Bill's job will only last for two months, it is called a _____ position.
9. Another name for a learner on a job is an _____ .
10. Melissa had to buy a _____ to wear when she worked as a waitress.
11. Most businesses must pay extra wages for the _____ hours that people work.
12. When George was given a _____ because of his good work, he also received a raise.
13. There were many _____ taken out of Julie's paycheck.
14. _____ is getting paid for one's work.

BANKING

savings account	a special account for money you are saving
interest	money paid by a bank for keeping money in a savings account
passbook	a book which keeps a record of your savings
deposit	to put money into the bank
withdrawal	taking money out of a savings account
checking account	a special account in a bank which lets you deposit money and write checks.
statement	a record of all the checks which you wrote, deposits you made, and any service charges during a certain time period.
service charge	amount charged by the bank for taking care of a checking account
overdraft	when you write a check for more money than you have in your checking account
endorse	sign your name on the back of a check so you can cash it
safe deposit box	a steel box rented to you by the bank for keeping important papers and valuables
bonds	a way to save money by buying government bonds (The government can use your money now and will return it, plus interest, at a later time.)
travelers checks	special checks bought at the bank so you don't have to carry lots of money on a trip (They must be signed at the bank when you buy them and endorsed when you cash them.)
balance	the amount of money that is in a checking account

On a separate sheet of paper, number from 1 to 16. Write the correct word for each blank from the list of banking words.

1. When you buy ______, you are letting the government use your money for a certain length of time.
2. It is safer to take ______ on vacation than to carry cash.
3. The banks sends you an ______ notice when you have written checks for more money than you have in your checking account.
4. Shelley must ______ her paycheck on the back when she cashes it.
5. To buy a car, John made a ______ from his savings account.
6. A ______ into your savings account means putting money into it.
7. Before Vince wrote checks to pay his bills, he made sure he had enough money in his ______.
8. At the end of the month, a ______ was sent to Vince with a list of all the checks he had written, the deposits he had made, the service charges, and his new balance.
9. Tasha wanted to save money, so she opened a ______ at the bank.
10. The more money you put into a savings account, the more ______ the bank adds to your account.
11. You need to bring your ______ to the bank with you when you make a deposit so that you can have a record of your savings.
12. Ms. Hughes put her valuable coin collection into a ______ before she went on her vacation.
13. A small amount charged by the bank for keeping records of your checking account is called a ______.
14. The money left in your checking account after subtracting the amount of a check you wrote is called the ______.

LAW

bench	the place where a judge sits
plaintiff	person who brings a matter to court
defendant	person against whom a matter is brought to court
attorney	lawyer
case	something that requires a decision in court; a lawsuit
witness	a person who knows something about a case and tells what he or she knows in court
testimony	what is said by a witness in court
oath	a promise to tell the truth in court
evidence	proof
jury	people selected to listen to a case and make a final decision
verdict	the final decision in a case
acquit	to free
exonerate	to declare not guilty; to set free a punishment given by a judge
sentence	a punishment given by a judge
pardon	to release a person from punishment; to forgive
parole	being freed from prison before the end of a sentence on the condition of continued good behavior
capital punishment	put someone to death as a punishment

On a separate sheet of paper, number from 1 to 15. Write the correct word for each blank from the list of **law** words.

1. The prisoner was given a ______ because of his good behavior.
2. A lawsuit is called a ______ .
3. The lawyer, or ______, asked the witness many important questions.
4. The ______ of each witness is very important to a case.
5. The judge listened to the case while he was sitting on the ______ .
6. The woman put her hand on the Bible and took an ______ to tell the truth while she was a witness.
7. Proof given in court is called ______ .
8. Two words that both mean to free are ______ and ______ .
9. If the jury reaches a verdict of guilty, the judge will give out a ______ .
10. Putting people to death for committing crimes, called ______, has been outlawed in most states.
11. Because the man was dying, the judge granted him a ______ so that he would not have to spend his last days in prison.
12. Because the woman had seen the accident, she was called as a ______ .
13. The ______ brings a matter to court and accuses someone of doing something wrong.
14. ______ try to defend themselves by proving that they are innocent.
15. The ______, which is made up of citizens living in a certain area, must decide if the defendant is guilty or not guilty. The jury's decision is called the ______.

SPACE

re-entry	coming back to earth's atmosphere after space travel
mission	a trip into space
launching pad	raised stand that is used when a rocket is sent into space
orbit	to go around in a circular movement
astronaut	a person who travels in space
capsule	small sealed container for space flight
solar system	the sun and its planets
countdown	counting backward aloud to show how much time is left before a launch
blast off	a rocket taking off for a space flight

On a separate sheet of paper, number from 1 to 8. Write the correct word for each blank from the list of **space** words.

1. At Cape Kennedy in Florida, the ______ began "10—9—8—7—6 . . . . . "
2. After the countdown reaches 1, you can hear the exciting words, " ______ ."
3. When the rocket takes off, everyone watchs the platform, which is called the ______ .
4. Dressed in a space suit, the ______ looked a little strange.
5. Earth is a planet in our ______ , and it revolves around the sun.
6. Project Apollo was the first ______ to take Americans to the moon.
7. The flight of a space ship in a circular movement is called an ______ .
8. When a small space capsule comes back into the earth's atmosphere, it is called ______ .

ECOLOGY

recycle	to use raw materials again to prevent the waste of resources
pollution	dangerously dirty conditions
litter	junk or garbage thrown on the ground
conservation	careful use of resources to save some for later use
natural resources	things such as forests, minerals, and water that man needs to live
environment	your surroundings
wildlife	animals living in natural areas
habitat	the home of wildlife
extinct	certain kinds of plants and animals that no longer exist.
erosion	the wearing away of soil by wind and water

On a separate sheet of paper, number from 1 to 10. Write the correct word for each blank from the list of **ecology** words.

1. When the wind and water wear away the soil, it is called ______.
2. When we buy pop in returnable bottles, the bottles can be ______.
3. It is very ugly to see ______ thrown along our highways.
4. It is healthier and more beautiful to live in a clean ______.
5. The bald eagle and the buffalo are protected by the United States so they will not become ______.
6. Water, forests, coal, and oil are some of our country's ______.
7. ______ of the air can cause lung diseases.
8. ______ can make sure that our natural resources will still be here many years from now.
9. Deer and racoons are examples of ______.
10. The forest is the ______ of many wild animals.

MEDICINE AND HEALTH

tablets	flat pills
drowsy	tired
sedative	medicine that helps a person relax and feel less pain
innoculation	shot given to prevent a certain disease
contagious	easily spread from one person to another
virus	something very small that causes diseases
symptom	a sign that something is wrong with your body
blood pressure	the pressure of the blood against the walls of the blood vessels
deficiency	a shortage of something
antibiotic	medicine used to destroy germs which are causing a disease

On a separate sheet of paper, number from 1 to 10. Write the correct word for each blank from the list of **medicine** words.

1. The doctor gave Margaret an ______ to kill the germs that were making her sick.
2. Rick took two ______ for his headache.
3. The doctor said her illness was caused by a tiny ______ .
4. When my mother had a check up, the doctor took her ______ to make sure it wasn't too high.
5. The label on the cold medicine said it might make you so ______ that you shouldn't drive a car.
6. A high temperature can be a ______ of a serious disease.
7. She was in so much pain that the doctor gave her a ______ so she could sleep.
8. Jim needed an ______ against diphtheria before he could go to South America.
9. Measles is a very ______ disease.
10. We take vitamins to prevent a vitamin ______.

OCCULT

astrology	a study of the effects of the stars, planets, and moon on people's lives
astrologer	a person who practices astrology
zodiac	a division of the heavens into twelve parts
sign	a symbol for each of the twelve parts of the zodiac
horoscope	telling future events according to astrology and the signs of the zodiac
clairvoyant	a person who has the special power to see into the future
predict	tell what is going to happen in the future
ESP	the abbreviation for extrasensory perception, which means to receive knowledge from other means besides the five senses

On a separate sheet of paper, number from 1 to 7. Write the correct word for each blank from the list of **occult** words.

1. The sense which lets people communicate without talking is called ______.
2. A person who studies the effects of stars, planets, and the moon on human life is called an ______.
3. To find out what might happen to you tomorrow, you could read your ______ in the newspaper.
4. Because Jerry's birthday is February 25th, his ______ of the zodiac is Pisces.
5. The study of the effects of the stars, planets, and the moon on human life is called ______.
6. The ______ divides the heavens into twelve parts.
7. People who have ESP can sometimes ______ things that will happen in the future. When they do this, they are called ______.

TRAVEL

itinerary	a list of places that a person plans to visit on a trip
scenic route	a route which is pretty and offers many things to see
tourist	a person who is traveling for pleasure while on vacation
tour	a planned trip which will take people to many interesting places
departure	leaving
cruise	taking a boat trip for pleasure
excursion	a trip offered at reduced prices
package deal	a special deal with transportation, tours, hotels and meals included in price
American plan	hotel charges that include room and meals in the one price
European plan	hotel charges for room only

On a separate sheet of paper, number from 1 to 10. Write the correct word for each blank from the list of **travel** words.

1. Before visiting Japan, we planned the ______ carefully.
2. The plane's ______ is 12:45, so we will have to hurry.
3. People who want to pay one price for both their hotel room and their food can choose the ______.
4. People who want to eat in restaurants outside of their hotel will choose the ______.
6. It took us an extra hour, but the ______ was so beautiful that it was worth the extra time.
6. A ______ in France might have a few difficulties if he or she doesn't speak French.
7. On his first trip to Europe, Bob chose a ______ so he wouldn't have to worry about where to stay or where to eat.
8. An ______ is a trip offered at reduced prices.
9. An ocean ______ is a relaxing trip on a ship.

10. There were thirty people who went with us on the ______ of Mexico City and the surrounding area.

FRENCH WORDS IN A RESTAURANT

menu	a list of the foods which are served
café	a small restaurant
soup du jour	the soup of the day
a la carte	a separate price for each thing ordered—not a complete dinner
au jus	served in the natural juices
entrée	the main part of the meal
buffet	many dishes set out on a long table where people can serve themselves
chef	a cook
a la mode	served with ice cream
maitre 'd	the head waiter

On a separate sheet of paper, number from 1 to 10. Write the correct word for each blank from the list of **French** words.

1. The waiter said that onion soup was the ______.
2. There was so much on the ______ that we couldn't decide what to order.
3. The small restaurant was called The French ______.
4. The ______ often wears a white hat in the kitchen.
5. If you are not hungry enough to eat a whole dinner, you could order your food ______.
6. Roast beef served with its natural juices is called ______.
7. For my ______, I ordered roast duck and a baked potato.
8. The restaurant has a ______ every night, where people can serve themselves and eat all they want.
9. For dessert, Terry had apple pie with a scoop of vanilla ice cream, which is called pie ______.
10. The ______ took us to our table and introduced our waiter.

FOREIGN WORDS

bon voyage	French for have a good trip
adios	Spanish for good bye
amigo	Spanish for friend
amour	French for love
gesundheit	German for good health, it is said when someone sneezes
chauffeur	French for a person hired to drive for someone
kosher	Yiddish for proper
moccasins	American Indian for a soft leather type of shoes
patio	Spanish for paved area near back of house

On a separate sheet of paper, number from 1 to 8. Write the correct word for each blank from the list of **foreign** words.

1. Carl liked to wear ______ around his house, instead of his regular shoes.
2. They were so rich that they hired a ______ to drive.
3. Before Carolyn left for Europe, we gave her a ______ party.
4. It was fun to sit on the ______ to cool off on hot summer evenings.
5. I said, "______", when Mrs. Grant sneezed.
6. The song used the word ______ , which is French for love.
7. It is not ______ to cheat on a test.
8. In Spanish, you would call a friend an ______ and say ______ instead of good-bye.

YOUR VOCABULARY

In this chapter, you have learned many new words. But, your vocabulary is still not complete. The English language is constantly growing by adding new words. And, as we have new experiences, we come in contact with more new words. Learning new words is a part of everyday living.

INDEX